Boscastle

16 August 2004

the day of the flood

David Rowe

Published by Truran November 2004
Reprinted December 2004, April 2005, July 2005, July 2006,
July 2007, July 2009, March 2011

Truran is an imprint of Truran Books Ltd
Goonance, Water Lane, St Agnes, Cornwall TR5 0RA
www.truranbooks.co.uk

ISBN 978 185022 193 7

The author & publishers would like to thank the many people who have kindly allowed them
to use their photographs for this book. Ownership is acknowledged in each caption.
Front cover – Aaron Wood   Inside front cover – Kerriann Godwin
Back cover – Don Stollery   Inside back cover – Don Stollery
Title page – Rick Barnett
Where there is no acknowledgement the photograph was taken by the author.
The copyright of all these images remains with the owners and may not be used
without their consent.

Printed and bound in Cornwall by Active Colour, Pool Industrial Park, Wilson Way, Redruth,
Cornwall TR15 3RX

The author, David Rowe, contributed a percentage of his royalties to the North
Cornwall Flood Appeal, which was set up to help those people affected by the flood.
The publishers matched this figure and to date £7000 has been contributed. In all
nearly half a million pounds was raised.

The fund was closed in 2007, and our continued contribution was transferred to
the Parish Council to be used to assist various organisations and groups in the
village. The author and pubishers continue too support this new fund for the
benefit of all in Boscastle.

This account is a snapshot of the great flood of August 16, 2004, and concentrates mainly on
Boscastle because that is where the majority of the 100 airlifts were carried out. The author and
publishers acknowledge that other communities in the surrounding area saw acts of
considerable bravery and also suffered terrible damage. They, too, are still in the long process of
recovery. We are sure their stories will be told in time.

FOREWORD

On August 16, 2004, Mother Nature unleashed one of Britain's worst rainstorms in living memory on the hills above our beloved Boscastle. The village is held very dearly by all those who have ever visited and those who live and work here, especially people like myself who have lived all our lives in this beautiful place. This book tells the story of that terrible day – the people in danger, the rescues, the damage caused by the sheer force of the speeding water and the debris carried by it. We who were here that Monday will never forget the way people of the village, many of whom suffered such damage to their homes and businesses, pulled together to help those less fortunate than themselves, and the courage and resilience of those in danger and their rescuers.

As I write this two months on, it is so encouraging to see two shops and a pub already reopened, and part of the Old Mill to open very shortly. I am sure Easter 2005 will see many more open. As we look towards a bright future, we in Boscastle will never forget that day and how the actions of so many typified the spirit of this special village.

George Findlay, Chairman of Forrabury and Minster Parish Council.

October 2004.

(Myrna Lester)

3

'Pass to all emergency services. This is a major incident. I repeat. This a major incident. We require all standby aircraft available and all available land-based emergency crews as we are in danger of losing Boscastle and all the people in it.'

Message timed at 5.10 pm, August 16, 2004, to RAF Kinloss Aeronautical Rescue Co-ordination Centre from Captain Pete McLelland (Royal Marines), flying above Boscastle, North Cornwall, in Royal Navy Sea King Helicopter 193.

(Aaron Wood)

*This book is dedicated to the people in Boscastle
and beyond, whose courage
and quick thinking on August 16, 2004, meant
that not a single human life was lost on the day of
the flood. All of them made
'The Miracle' happen.*

THE DAY OF THE FLOOD

A MAGICAL PLACE

Nothing about the bright morning of August 16, 2004, suggested that Boscastle was about to see the greatest airlift on mainland Britain since the Second World War.

Beyond slate-black cliffs, the sea was a sheet of near-Mediterranean green. Just inland, sunlight sparkled on the Valency, Jordan, Paradise and Butts Water, and the other thin but nameless streams trickling down the hillsides. The many rivulets provide a soothing background music to the even pace of life in this North Cornwall backwater.

The ancient village, where people first settled more than 3,000 years ago, has three pubs, one primary school, two churches, and a museum housing the world's largest collection of witchcraft artefacts. It is a place fairly at peace with itself where people are known colloquially by their first names and what they do. Farmer Kev, Nev the baker and Raymund the artist are a few of the friendly figures you might pass the time of day with. The inhabitants are very loyal to Boscastle, describing it as a close, resilient community where people look out for each other. Some go as far as to call it a magical place.

The village and its people were familiar to television viewers who had followed the fortunes of the Rev Christine Musser, in the gentle BBC series *A Seaside Parish*. There were no great dramas – and that was part of the charm. Boscastle was an undoubted star of the show as the camera lingered lovingly on the heady coastline, lush valley and quaint streets.

Monday August 16 started out a pleasant, sunny day in North Cornwall. Around midday this huge black cloud was seen over the Camel Estuary, heading towards the hills above Boscastle (Barbara Kilby)

As the resident population of about a thousand went about its high summer business on that Monday morning, their number would be doubled, perhaps even trebled, by shoals of visitors flowing into the hilly streets. They would be drawn down to where the streams become a single waterway running between old harbour walls to meet the sea in the sinuous fjord that leads to the ocean. On a typical summer's day the river is little more than a pleasant trout stream.

Carole Talboys

Visitors meander along its banks, in and out of gift shops, bars and restaurants. Cornwall's notoriously fickle skies had made for a so-far wretched August but the village had escaped the worst of the weather and business was good. That unremarkable morning, Ken Cave, skipper of the *Boscastle Peganina*, welcomed a party of Somerset anglers on board. In its 19th century heyday, Boscastle was a commercial port dealing in coal and ironwork. Now the *Peganina* was the only big boat working out of the place. The sunshine, warming the deck as the skipper navigated through the clear waters of the dog-leg harbour and out past Meachard Rock, would last most of the day out at sea.

SCATTERED SHOWERS, BECOMING HEAVY IN THE AFTERNOON

Those who checked the regional weather forecast in the *Western Morning News* would have read that scattered showers would begin to form by the end of the morning, becoming heavy in places through the afternoon. The headline on a news story accompanying a picture of a family frolicking in the surf said: 'More unsettled weather on the way.' In the *Happened Today* column was a paragraph referring to a catastrophic event 69 miles along the Atlantic Highway where the topography is similar to Boscastle's. It read: 1952: 'Severe thunderstorms in Somerset and North Devon caused rivers to flood and devastated the towns of Lynton and Lynmouth.'

Carole Talboys doesn't call it a premonition but she had a weird experience on the morning of August 16, 2004. She was working as a volunteer at the Museum of Witchcraft on the north side of the harbour and walking past the crystal balls of the divination display when it happened. 'I know it's a strange thing to say but I felt something really odd,' she said. 'It was like somebody blew down my bare arms, either side of me, at one particular point. I passed that point several times on purpose and it happened every time.' She mentioned it to Graham King, the owner of the museum. They often swap stories of strange happenings. She then thought no more of it until much later.

A BIG BLACK CLOUD

About midday, further down the Cornish coast at St George's Well on the Camel Estuary, Barbara Kilby, a visitor from Bexhill-on-Sea, had a more obvious sense of foreboding when she looked up at what had been a clear blue sky. 'It was frightening,' she said. 'We were on a bright, sunlit beach and the sky was as blue as blue. It was a beautiful day. We had hot sunshine. And then there was this great black wedge of cloud. It was extraordinary. I have never seen a cloud like this before. I said to my daughter "Somebody's going to get a downpour." Later on we saw all the helicopters go by. We didn't even realise then it was a disaster. We thought it was an exercise.'

The flood builds up at the second bridge. At this point the rushing water was still a spectator sport but soon the first car would shoot down and crash into the bridge. That started a huge build-up of vehicles and trees which would force the torrent sideways, causing massive damage to buildings either side of the river (Kerriann Godwin)

The seven-mile deep flank of bruised cumulonimbus was heading up the coast to take up position on the high ground above the deep, narrow V of the Valency Valley. The noted beauty spot would become a conduit for millions of tons of water that afternoon, a phenomenal deluge that would leave the pleasant stream at its bottom looking more like a Canadian river. At one point the emergency services believed as many as 1,000 people could be lost. Then in came a team of helicopters since dubbed 'The Magnificent Seven' – three from the RAF, three from the Navy, and one from the Coastguard. Because the valley is so narrow, only one aircraft at a time could fly into and pluck the cold and frightened from the rooftops and out of the skylights of Boscastle. In total 100 people and a dog were airlifted from the lower village and beyond, a monumental mission which will go down in Search and Rescue history as one of the finest ever, one that would become known as 'The Miracle of Boscastle'.

TIME MELTED ON AUGUST 16

From the time that brilliant morning yielded to a dark, threatening, eerie afternoon of lightning, thunder, monsoon rain and hail – even glimpses of sunshine – hours, minutes and seconds seem to have melted for many of the people in Boscastle and the surrounding area. Ask them just when the clouds burst, when the power went off, when they first heard the bomb-like crack of a dam of trees breaching and the scream of the river, or saw

The day the roads became rivers: A group of ramblers march purposefully up steep Fore Street against the downcoming torrent unaware of the impending danger (Aaron Wood)

it change from a chuckling, translucent brook to a lethal, gloopy torrent – some say it was like chocolate, others that it was graphite black – and they will say they can't really be sure. Ask them when it was they saw that first red car shoot down and smash into the second bridge, or when the phones went dead and there was no way they could call their loved ones trapped in the flood, or when their front doors were punched open by fists of water, or when they craned their necks and watched their small, frightened children ascend into helicopters, and they will say 'Sorry, we can't be exact.'

This was a day a young singer-songwriter was washed out of a cottage and into the street by the invading water and shouted for her life as she clung to a drainpipe, convinced the flood would take her away. This was a day when a boy screamed 'We are all going to die now ' – as his mother tried to calm him, though she had the same fear in her heart. This was a day when senior firefighters tried to reassure women and children penned in by water running past first-floor windows that everything would be OK – while they secretly thought they would never see their own wives and children again. This was a day when Search and Rescue crewmen – some of them war veterans – looked down on the torrent in disbelief and feared many would be lost. And yet at the end of few hours of mayhem, all were saved.

So unreal were the scenes played out before so many pairs of eyes that people used film analogies to describe what they saw. One witness, an experienced pilot, described the view from the air as like a Bruce Willis action movie. Another, a senior paramedic, said the swarm of helicopters reminded him of a Vietnam war film.

A man who watched in amazement as water smashed through the back of Boscastle Bakery and washed everything – including a giant oven – out the front described it as like a scene from *Titanic*. Many used the words surreal, strange and bizarre. More than one described the floodwaters as evil. Eight inches of rain fell on roads and hillsides and at the height of the flood more than 100 tons of water were funnelling through Boscastle every second. First it smelt of the earth and huge trees it had ripped like weeds from the valley. Then it reeked of the fuel that poured from cars tossed about like plastic ducks. Several reported the levels rising and then strangely dipping two, maybe three times. Then there was the noise. The calming symphony of the streams turned into a hideous cacophony of roars and bangs. Thomas Hardy's 'wild weird western shore' can never have been wilder or weirder than this.

Graham King

Necessarily, the accounts here cannot follow a strict chronology, because of the sheer number of life-threatening events being played out simultaneously. By the late evening there were thousands of shocked witnesses. Many have found the best way to deal with the trauma is to talk it over with someone else who was there and understands the ferocity of the flood. Some people are still suffering nightmares in which the flood comes again.

LIKE A FIERCE KETTLE, SUDDENLY BOILING

And so the rain came in. By 1.15 pm it was torrential. The poor weather drove yet more holidaymakers off the beaches and moorlands and down into the village streets. Just as sunshine is a magnet to the sands, when it rains in North Cornwall, Boscastle teems. As the afternoon wore on, shops and eating places were doing good business. The car park by the visitor centre had about 170 spaces and by three o'clock was nearly full. Down river by the second and more picturesque of the bridges, Graham King was sitting in his upstairs office while Carole Talboys oversaw the now extremely busy museum. Carole said: 'I had a booth full of people waiting to come in because of the rain and I heard a noise like a really fierce kettle suddenly boiling, like a

roaring noise, in the click of a finger.

'I went outside. The river was running black and very fast. I've never seen it look like that before. A man standing on the bridge turned to me and said there had been a big wave coming down the river.'

Graham saw that it was unusually high. He said: 'In summer it's usually just a very pretty little stream. There have been trout in it this year. We've been sitting outside the Riverside Hotel watching them in the river.'

He tried to phone his partner Kerriann Godwin, who was in her cottage on the other side of the river near the Wellington Hotel. But he couldn't get through so her sent her an email (timed at 3.04 pm) saying 'Go and have a look at the river.'

'I could see some of the people who have lived here a long time were getting on edge. That put me on edge as well,' he said.

By around 3.30 pm, the river was level with the banks. Carole was disturbed by what she was seeing. She said: 'I thought it was really weird. This first bit was black, or like a really really dark brown peat, racing in the water.'

She looked out again and saw a woman and child on the slipway nearby, inches from the water: 'I said to Graham about it and he grabbed his coastguard jacket. Just then the water started to spill over and it was coming down each side of the bridge.'

WE'VE GOT AN INCIDENT DEVELOPING IN BOSCASTLE

As well as being owner of the museum, Graham is Deputy Station Officer for Boscastle Coastguard. He said: 'It was dangerous down there so I put my coastguard jacket on. It just gives me a bit of authority – I wanted to warn them off. I ran down and as I was going back in the river had burst its banks. There was another woman and a little baby trying to walk upstream against the torrent. I told them in no uncertain terms

The flood cascades down Fore Street. This picture was taken about half an hour after those on page 8. Note how the red car has swung around in the force of the flood (Rick Barnett)

they were being stupid and to get up to higher ground. I then went and phoned Falmouth Coastguards and told them "We've got an incident developing in Boscastle." '

Records show that call was at 3.44 pm – the official start of the massive rescue mission.

By the time Graham crossed the second bridge it was knee-deep in water. He was the last to get across it that day. He phoned Falmouth again and asked them to page the rest of the team. He then got the coastguard vehicle from the coastguard station on the river bank because he knew it would soon be enveloped in water. He drove up to the first bridge at the hub of lower Boscastle.

He said: 'By then it was a raging torrent. I was totally on my own, the only person in uniform in the whole of Boscastle, which was a bit nerve-racking. The other problem is we don't have radio communications out of here between us and Falmouth because we are in a steep valley. I called them again on the mobile phone. I made it very clear that I wanted helicopters and lots of help. The message was short and to the point!

'All I could do was a bit of crowd control. I was recruiting any face I recognised that was local. I was giving them incident tape. We were just cordoning off areas. I couldn't do any more than that. They were all honorary lifesavers.'

RIP TIDES AND CURRENTS CHURNED BETWEEN CARS

Scott Roberts is head chef of the Wellington Hotel, owned by his parents Paul and Rose. On the afternoon of August 16, he was surfing at Widemouth Bay, 12 miles from Boscastle, when he noticed a big black cloud coming up the coast. When the rain came steaming down, Scott left the water, changed

Cars and camper vans float around Boscastle car park after the River Valency burst its banks. Many vehicles would be washed down the main street and into the harbour. Seventy-nine were later recovered from the lower village and inner and outer harbour areas (Don Stollery)

out of his wetsuit and drove towards home. As he came into Boscastle there was a lot of traffic coming out of the village. People were signalling for him to turn back around but he carried on down towards the car park. He parked beside it and quickly saw that the River Valency had burst its banks.

Scott said: 'I noticed a woman over by the bottle banks, out of a car, and she was screaming. I thought "Right, I'll go and get her." I put my wetsuit on, jumped over the wall and went in. The water was up to my shins at that point and I walked her out. She had been frightened by the flood.'

As the spreading floodwater rapidly became much deeper and faster, Scott went back into the car park and guided more people out. Very soon it was up to waist height and cars and the bottle banks started to move around. There were little islands in the car park with people stuck on them, too scared to move, and some

of those, too, were helped out by Scott.

He then saw people stuck in a car at the top of the car park. He said: 'I got about 100 yards away from them and they were climbing out. As they were getting out a little girl of about six or seven fell out of the car and got swept into the water. I went running as fast as I could and caught her. I lost my footing and starting swimming against the current. It was hard to stand up. I got my footing on one of these little islands and got her up on my shoulders and waded across the car park and put her down.'

After assisting the girl, Scott went back into the torrent and carried out another young girl and an elderly woman. In all, he helped around ten people to safety.

Another man whose quick thinking and selfless actions helped others was a visitor on holiday from Gloucestershire with his family.

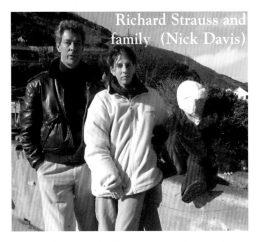
Richard Strauss and family (Nick Davis)

Richard and Rachelle Strauss and their three-year-old daughter Verona had arrived in the car park and parked at the top end at about 3.50 pm. They waited for the rain to ease off before running into the newsagents to buy some crayons and paper to entertain Verona in the wet weather.

As they browsed in the shop, Richard heard a low rumble and went outside to find the car park covered in brown, fast-flowing water. He decided they should leave immediately and after much difficulty they drove out of the car park and stopped on higher ground. Richard could see that people were in danger so he ran back to the car park.

He recalled: 'People just stood around looking amazed and shocked. The water was rising rapidly. I could see rip tides and churning current between cars and already there was water half way up the tyres and over the door sills. The car park was still about 80 per cent full and lots of people were trying to drive through churning waters towards the entrance.'

He managed to escort some people to the safety of the shop. Then he spotted a car towards the lower, deeper end. The flood water was covering the tyres. Richard said: 'There was a woman with her head out of the sunroof screaming for help. It was a heart-stopping moment. I would have to cross the main torrent of water to reach her and by now there was larger debris and rubbish skips floating around and crashing into cars.

'I shouted to the stranded car that we were coming to help. In true British spirit other people had heard my call and realised this was the time for real action. About three of us linked arms and finally made it to the car. The woman was still screaming for help. In the car were two other women. They were unable to open the doors because of the water level and strong current were pressing them closed. We managed to hold open the passenger door and drag the one frightened woman out. Somehow the other men managed to get her safely to the high ground while I stayed with the other two. They were dazed and pale, clearly shocked and unable to deal with the situation. We got the second woman out and to safety and I shouted to the last woman, the driver. "We've got to go NOW, leave it, it's all covered with the insurance."

'I saw a true look of fear and horror in her eyes as she slowly gave me her hand. She felt weak and powerless and I could see that she

Dave 'College' Fletcher

12

was overwhelmed. As she stepped out she slipped and fell in the water. I didn't even think but reacted to catch her by letting go of my own anchor-hold. I've never seen anyone move so fast and totally out of control. Thankfully I was down stream and just caught her as she was passing my legs. The other men immediately held us both and we made our way to safety.' The three men now worked as a team helping others to safety.

When the Strauss family drove out of Boscastle, the car park was still about 60 per cent full.

IT WOULD HAVE BEEN CARNAGE

At the bridge, Graham King was relieved to find help was at hand in the form of Dave 'College' Fletcher. He lives up the hill from the harbour at Fore Street where he runs the guest house Myrtle Cottage with his partner Molly Webber. At around 4 o'clock he got a call from a friend at the bottom of the village asking if he had any sandbags.

College drove down to the bridge where he saw Graham in the coastguard vehicle with the light flashing. College – the name started as a mickey–take when he was an apprentice mechanic – recalled: 'Graham came along with the blue and white cordon tape and I manned the cordon, stopping people going on to the bridge. But there were people still coming around the corner, getting away from the shops.'

Then the cars started coming down on the flood.

College said: 'The first was a red Ford. It went straight underneath the bridge. It was definitely speeding. Quite a few cars came down with their hazards on. I was trying to see if there was anyone in them but I didn't have

my glasses on. The fire brigade turned up. At that point it was bucketing down and everyone was going into the 'Welly' (the Wellington Hotel). People were really crammed into the entrance way. You had to push to get past them all at the bar – it's called the Long Bar. They were still serving drinks. I ordered a double brandy to give myself a quick shot.'

College knows the layout of the Wellington well from working there ten years before as a chef. While most visitors were mesmerised by the spreading Valency, few would have known what he knew – that the Jordan flows right underneath the 400-year-old hotel through a culvert before it meets its sister river.

College said: 'I found Paul (Roberts) the owner who was out the back. I walked out and looked at the culvert. You could hear the water splashing on the top really torrential. I said to Paul "We've got to get everyone out."

Shortly after the Long Bar of the Wellington Hotel was evacuated, the River Jordan smashed through the back of the premises and poured out the front, causing massive damage (Rick Barnett)

I said "Everyone's got to leave the bar, nice and calmly, no panic." We knew the place was going to flood. I just got everyone out by really loudly addressing them. Shouting in a measured way. It was absolutely tipping down. People weren't keen.'

There might have been a waver in College's voice – but they obeyed him anyway. The occupants of the Long Bar came out the front and most went up the hill leading to the hairpin bend.

Paul Roberts and son Scott's girlfriend Suzanne Harari went upstairs to clear the hotel. Around six rooms had people in them and they were safely evacuated.

A few minutes after the Wellington was cleared, thousands of tons of water, rocks and mud rammed through the first floor windows at the back, smashing through the wooden floor and filling the bar where people had been standing.

Paul said that all the beams in the bar had been smashed: 'There was about 13 feet of water and 120 tons of mud.' Paul and Suzanne were the last to leave the building through a side exit on the first floor.

College said: 'The whole of the back of the Wellington had become a dam and when the dam burst it came through the ceiling and burst through the whole bar into the river channel. Had anyone been in there it would have been carnage. I had no idea it would smash the whole place to bits in one fell swoop.'

College reversed his car up the hill part of the way home until it was pushed to the side of the road by the cascading water. The hilly streets had turned into rivers. He got out and started running. He was hit by debris and a week later his shins would still show the cuts he sustained that day. When he got back home he found the cottage running in water.

He said: 'It was pouring in. Molly was on the phone. Water was coming in the front and going out the back. The sound was unbelievable. It was deafening. People couldn't get across and down the road. Our neighbours' cars were both washed down the road.'

I CLUNG ONTO THE DRAINPIPE. I THOUGHT 'I'M GOING TO DIE.' AND I THINK I SWORE. LOADS

Emily Maughan was alone and asleep when the water began to nudge at the front door of the Valency Row cottage she shares with her boyfriend Sam Washer. The narrow, cobbled thoroughfare on the opposite side of the river to the Wellington is the original passageway to the harbour and one of the oldest parts of Boscastle. The 24-year-old had been waiting tables at the Cobweb Inn just up the road and finished her split shift at 3 pm. It had not been the best of days. She had fallen over at work while carrying a plate of chips and walloped her elbow. The job was just a fill-in while Emily, a talented singer-songwriter, hoped for a serious break into the music business. Singing is in her blood. Her father

Emily Maughan

John is a builder by trade but is better known for his big hat and big baritone voice as the 'Boscastle Busker'.

Emily said: 'I went to sleep just listening to the rain. My boyfriend rang me at quarter past four and I was a bit disorientated.' Sam asked Emily if she had looked outside and when she peered down from the bedroom window she could see the flood running down Valency Row.

'He said "Can you get out?" I said "Of course I can get out. Don't worry." I went downstairs. I got to the front door and I was standing in water. I went and looked out the kitchen window and realised I couldn't actually get out at all.'

Emily then rang her mother Cheryl. The Maughan family home is high up on the other side of the river. Emily said: 'I said to mum "I can't get out of the house." She set off with a broom to unblock my drain! She is very like me, my mum!'

This would be the last call Emily would make for many hours. As the water started to shoot in around the frame of the solid-wood front door, she got a bucket and bailed it down the sink.

She said: 'It wasn't just the bottom of the door, it was coming through further up and I thought "This really is quite bad." I started to have a little panic. Then the last thing I remember is putting my hand up on the door. I held it. Then it came off both hinges. The door just flew towards me and a tidal wave of water came over the top. It was heavy anyway so I fell right back with it on top of me. I tried to push the door off me and I was underneath the water. I think the current pushed me back out of the house. One minute I was underneath the door and the water, then I came up for air and I was outside the house. Then I saw the rest of the village. I had no

idea of how bad it was. I saw an enormous river, the whole of the village covered. The water stank. It was like a really earthy muddy smell. Everything was covered. There were 12 people standing on the stairs of the Cornish Stores (across the deeply-flooded road). They were all shouting at me.'

Though shoeless, somehow Emily managed to find her footing in the chest-deep surge. 'So I start to try and get to the people but they were actually telling me not to go to them. Earlier

John Maughan

there were tourists everywhere. They had all disappeared except for these people and this torrent of water. I was being whacked back into the wall. It was like 50-60 miles an hour. I must have just completely freaked. I don't like being underwater anyway. I'm a good swimmer but I couldn't have swum in that.'
Struggling into the flow, she managed to get past her front door and a couple of paces along the wall, where she clung to her neighbour's drainpipe. 'Luckily it was a metal one and stuck fast. I screamed and screamed and screamed. I thought 'If someone doesn't come out soon I'm going to get washed down this river.' And I think I swore. Loads. I was weakening. With the shock of being under the water and the shock of seeing no-one

there to help me, I though "I'm going to die." I really really did. It was so fast, the water. I could see that there was nowhere you could go. The only way I thought I could go was to shout, or just get carried along towards the sea and scream all the way down. I was just going to scream until somebody helped me.'

I REMEMBER THINKING 'I BET THERE'S 50 DROWNED TONIGHT'

John McLaughlin and drainpipe

The roar of the flood and the clatter of a helicopter meant Emily's screams could not have carried so far as the other side of the water to the hairpin bend. There her mother and boyfriend peered anxiously across the torrent in the direction of the cottage. Fortunately, her cries would be heard by someone nearer by.

Earlier that afternoon Emily's father John had been working on a conservatory in Tintagel four miles from Boscastle when the sky went black. Within ten minutes the road was six-inches deep in flood water. He phoned his wife Cheryl and told her it was rain like he'd never seen. He said: 'Three or four times in the afternoon it deluged for about ten minutes but most of the time it was sunny and hot. It was going from extreme to extreme. All the time from half one onwards there was this huge black cloud over Davidstow, the moor inland from Tintagel and Boscastle. It just seemed to expand and contract.'

When Cheryl called him and told him about Emily's phone call saying she was trapped by the flood, he stopped work and drove home. He then sped down to the bottom of the village on his mountain bike.

He said: 'There was debris all over the road, boulders, mud. I pedalled down to the hairpin bend and found there was a crowd of people

there in a state of amazement. It was pouring down. You could barely see. The sky was black as night. There was lightning. I saw Cheryl fairly quickly and then looked over the wall. It's hard to find words to describe it. The power, the depth, the blackness of it. I've seen floods and they are always brown. This was absolutely jet black. It looked really evil. It was bringing tons and tons of soil down. I'm looking at this knowing my daughter is over the other side.'

John and Cheryl kept trying to ring Emily, youngest of their three children, on her mobile. They could hardly hear each other speak because the noise was so deafening.

John decided he must try to reach Emily so went home, grabbed a length of climbing rope, and tried to drive the long way round to the other side of the village. His plan was to lower himself down to the cottage from the bank above. With floods pouring off the steep fields, he managed to get as far as the A39 but could not drive any further because of the number of stationary cars.

Feeling powerless to reach his daughter, he then returned to the hairpin to find his wife. 'Cheryl looked dreadful. Obviously stressed,' said John. 'When buildings started collapsing, I was thinking of all these people waving out of their upstairs windows, that all their buildings would collapse as well. I remember thinking "I bet you there's 50 people drowned tonight." '

Unknown to her parents, by this time Emily had been saved from the flood thanks to the voice that has enthralled audiences from London to Cornwall – and the strong arms of her next-door neighbour.

I OPENED A BOTTLE OF WINE. THEN I HEARD SCREAMS

John McLaughlin was also at home alone in Valency Row. He too had finished work. He is joint manager of Boscastle AFC and knows Emily's boyfriend who also plays for the football club. John's wife Nadine was at work and he had been flicking between the Olympics and Test Cricket when the rain came down. By the time the water was running knee-deep in the street outside he had taken in two women he knew from the village who had sought refuge after walking through the rising waters from Things shop about 200 yards away.

John McLaughlin said: 'They were all right. I got the camera out and started taking a few photos out of the front window. Not long after that cars started coming down. They were all hitting the wall by the Cornish Stores. I opened a bottle of wine. I thought as we weren't going anywhere for a little while we would have a drink. I phoned Nadine. I said not to come home because it was getting a bit wet.'

Then he heard screams.

The famous red car, now firmly wedged under the second bridge. The Harbour Light is now only minutes away from total destruction (Don Stollery)

17

Alfie Biscombe

For the singer the flood was a life-changing event. She has since decided to give up waiting tables to concentrate on her music.

MY RUNNER BEANS DISAPPEARED BEFORE MY EYES

The Valency Valley is one of the largest blocks of woodland in North Cornwall. Normally in August the waterway which gives it its name would be a ten-feet wide, shin-deep stream you can wade across. By mid afternoon on August 16, a couple of miles inland from Boscastle, it was now a 50-yard wide, 15-feet deep torrent scouring away all in its path.

Alfie Biscombe has lived in the narrow valley for 50 years, 45 of them spent as gardener at the Old Rectory in St Juliot. He clearly remembers the great flood of 1958 which claimed a single life, that of Boscastle's bandmaster. But he had never seen water like this. Alfie was indoors with his wife May when the river began to shoot up. He said: 'We are about 25 feet from the river and we have a five-bar orchard gate below our house. We gauge the river from that. We saw it go over three bars, which we've seen before. Then it went over five bars. We began to get worried then. Actually we didn't have torrential rain. We had a few downpours but it wasn't pouring down all the time. The vegetable plot got the full force of the flood. My three rows of runner beans disappeared before my eyes. Then we saw the river coming up to our front gate. This was about five to eight feet higher than it had ever done before, even in 1958.'

He said: 'There were quite a few screaming then because there were cars moving about. Emily was the closest so I could hear her screaming – and she has a loud voice. I went to the top bedroom and looked down. I could see it was Emily holding on to the drainpipe. I know her quite well. I was shouting to her to stay there. I could see her trying to get forward. She wasn't getting anywhere because of the water.'

John knew what he had to do. He went downstairs and as he opened the front door, three feet of water gushed in and up his stairs. He was struck by the stench of fuel which had poured from the cars. Keeping his right hand on the doorframe, he grabbed Emily with his left and hauled her in.

'She was a bit hysterical,' said John. 'She was crying. I gave her a hug and said "Calm down. Don't worry about it." I rolled her a fag and gave her a beer and sat her down. I got her some towels.'

Emily recalled: 'I was so panicked I don't remember what I was doing. I was screaming and shaking and trying to explain to them what had just happened.' John and the women were stuck there for the next four hours. Emily said she didn't stop sobbing for the first three of them.

They put their boots and coats on and got the dog on a lead – then breathed a sigh of relief as the river dropped by a foot and a half. Alarmingly, ten minutes later it started to rise again, this time even quicker.

Alfie said: 'It was a terrible brown. I saw great trees going down the valley. It was terrifying to see. It was traumatic. We went to the back door and by that time the water was coming into the bathroom, kitchen and dining room about a foot high. It ruined everything. I lost two sheds and a greenhouse. Our neighbour rang up and said we could go there. We stayed down there until the flood receded. The worst part the next day was looking out and seeing the devastation.

Everything had changed.'

The Harbour Light – before (Cyber Scribe)

I WENT THROUGH THE FLOOD OF 1958. I KNEW WHAT IT WAS

Trixie Webster is Boscastle through and through. Her business the Harbour Light was a converted pigsty on the riverbank just down from the Witchcraft Museum. With its quaint sloping roofs and arched windows, it was perhaps the most photographed building in the village where Trixie was born, and a tourist attraction in its own right. Until the afternoon of the flood it sold postcards, gifts, high-quality nautical clothing and ice cream. It used to be known as the Pixie Shop until Trixie began to feel uncomfortable with the name, though many in the village still call it that. Trixie is a Christian and the quaint premises was also an outreach with books and Bibles.

– and after (Aaron Wood)

When she and her assistant Sarah Hancock heard the roar of the river that day, Trixie sensed what was happening. She said: 'It had been raining but the sun was out and we had been selling ice creams from the kiosk outside. I looked out. I had been through the last flood in 1958 and I knew what it was. The river, all of a sudden, instead of being fairly low, was up to the banks.'

Trixie Webster

By the time she evacuated the shop at around 3.30 pm it was raining heavily. She said: 'We locked the shop. We put storm boards up in front of the door. We locked the gates. We put thick boards down with sandbags, two deep.'

Both Sarah and Trixie moved their cars, then crossed the bridge. Trixie's house is just across the river. She said: 'I boiled the kettle, had a cup of tea, looked out of the kitchen window and I could not believe my eyes. This car came down the river and up-righted itself at the bridge. We were concerned there might be someone in it. Then a tree came behind it. And all of a sudden then the river took a different course and then I saw the river, instead of running down where it should, went towards the Harbour Light. It went over the wall and up to the higher garden. It burst open the door and then it burst open the windows at the back and then it poured out of the back. I could see it rising inside. I saw the stock floating and thrashing around inside.'

I LOOKED AND IT WAS THERE. I LOOKED AGAIN AND IT WAS GONE

When the water burst open the front door of Trixie's house and rushed in and up the stairs she decided it was time to leave quickly. The only escape route was through the patio at the back and up a ladder to higher ground. Trixie said: 'The level of the river had risen 20 feet. I was calm. I wasn't frightened.'

She didn't see the Harbour Light being taken by the water. Sarah did. She said: 'I looked and it was there. I heard a shout. Then I looked again and it was gone.' The building – which had stood there for more than 300 years – suddenly collapsed and was washed away. She was in shock for days afterwards.

THE BBC RANG. I COUNTED 14 CARS GO PAST AS I WAS ON THE PHONE

Shortly before Graham King made the call that started the rescue, his partner Kerriann Godwin came down to the museum to join Carole Talboys. They evacuated the museum, sending people up the back and away from the river, and turned the power off. They watched in disbelief as the torrent swept down trees, cars, tables and chairs from outside the Spinning Wheel restaurant, recycling bins, even a big tropical plant which span down the flood in its pot. At one point the edge of the flood pulled off one of Kerriann's sparkly slippers and they watched it race away.

Carole said: 'That first car coming down was a huge shock to us. It smashed into the bridge and stood up – nose down and boot up – and it was pinned against the bridge for the whole time.'

They saw the Harbour Light crumble. Carole said: 'All of a sudden it broke apart and went. It fragmented. It all spread out and just sank. We were thinking about Trixie and what a

Rebecca David

shame it was for her. I remember the sound of the trees as they were forced over and under the bridge. Cracking noises. I remember thinking "This is silly now. It should stop!" '

Kerriann said: 'The BBC rang and just as I was speaking to them the first red car came and bashed into the bridge. I counted 14 cars going past while I was on the phone to them. The BBC said "We'll have to record you, hold on." Then the electricity went out so my BBC debut was curtailed. This was about 4.30. Carole and I suddenly decided to leave because we both felt some shaking in the museum. We went out the back door and climbed up a couple of cliffs. There were some guys up there and they hoisted us up.'

THE WATER WAS A BLOOMING NUISANCE

The first building the flood hit when it reached Boscastle village was the visitor centre in the car park. The single-storey, barn-like building, owned and run by North Cornwall District Council, attracted as many as 1,000 visitors a day. Adjoining it at the back was a public toilet block. The lavatory roof was about six feet lower. When the river was rapidly rising, Rebecca David, the centre manager, was busy trying to help an Australian who needed a visa to go home via Russia. The problem was, lightning strikes kept cutting the power and each time it came on again she had to reboot the computer.

At about 3.45 pm Rebecca noticed water coming into the porch of the centre and rang the Environment Agency and the Fire Brigade.

With the doors now shut against the rising water, inside the centre were 12 people: Rebecca, a volunteer helper Beryl Walters, and two families on holiday in North

The visitor centre – before (Heulyn Lewis)

– and after (Charlie David)

Cornwall, Alan and Melanie Graham, of Benfleet, Essex, and their three daughters, twins Emily and Charlotte (eight), and Rebecca (six), and Andy and Kim Evans, of Newbury, Berkshire, and their children Carl (ten), Luke (eight) and Emily (six). The families didn't know each other at the time, though they would soon to forge a close bond. The six children were becoming increasingly anxious and some were tearful. Rebecca said: 'Inside we had a children's play area with a little low wall of about 18 inches high. The families were standing on the wall. I thought the water was a blooming nuisance. One of the first things I did was turn off the power.'

The view from the roof of the crumbling visitor centre as the flood water nears the level of the guttering. Six adults and six children were trapped in the building. Most ended up on the roof and that of the adjoining toilet block. In desperation the parents planned that if anyone were to be washed away, they would try to reach the tree where the two cars were stuck. (Melanie Graham)

The visitor centre was about ten years old, solidly built local stone. At the back of the building behind the counter was a small storage loft reached by a ladder. Rebecca pulled it down and sent the families up: 'Beryl Walters was at the top of the ladder and I was halfway up.'

The families were now trapped in this tiny, hot space. There were piles of stock, meaning little room for the group now trapped by the water rising against the grey walls outside. There were no chairs so the children sat on the floor and played with sticker books Rebecca had found for them. Trying to keep them calm, Kim made light of the situation. When they heard a fire engine she said: 'The firemen are here, we'll be fine now.'
Melanie was disturbed by the sound of debris thudding into the building: 'It was a banging noise. A horrendous noise. Like somebody bashing the door down.'

At about 4.15 pm a second wave of floodwater rammed into the centre and smashed open the doors. Water rushed in and over the four-feet high counter. Rebecca rang her husband Charlie, the council's Coast and Countryside Manager, on her mobile phone. She asked him to let the police know that they were in the building and the doors had cracked. Rebecca said: 'That was the last he heard because the phones went. He was trying all the little roads, all ways to get into the village but couldn't get in. I was thinking, "I suppose I'm in charge." If I kept calm then everybody else would. I told them that the police knew we were in there and everything would be OK.'

By then the building was a small island of six adults and six children in the spreading flood plane of the Valency. It was the first resistance to the dark torrent as it rolled giant boulders down the valley, ripped up roads and washed cars and trees like toys and toothpicks into the lower village.

WE SANG 'THE WIPERS ON THE BUS GO SWISH, SWISH, SWISH'. THERE WAS A CRACK. MOST OF THE BUILDING HAD COLLAPSED

By the time the first rescue helicopter flew into the valley, the occupants of the visitor centre were peering anxiously out of the one window in the loft as the water inside rose up almost to their feet.

Rebecca recalled: 'I was trying to play it down a bit. One father asked: "How strong is this building?" I said "It'll be fine. It was built to be bomb-proof." And then I could see this wall of brown water coming at us. There was

The flooded river reaches its height near the harbour, lapping the roof of Cornish Goodies, with the Museum of Witchcraft behind it. The roof was left with a tear where a car had been washed along it - testimony to just how high the water had risen (Don Stollery)

a table up there so I said "You all sit on the table." The children were nervous, agitated and weepy.'

Melanie recalls: 'It was raining quite heavily by then. We kept opening the window to let fresh air in but you couldn't keep it open because the rain was too heavy.'

To try to revive their spirits Rebecca, a mother of two children aged 20 and 18, suggested they sing a song: 'So we started singing "The wheels on the bus" – it was back to playschool days! I even had them singing "The wipers on the bus go swish, swish, swish." '

The verse was abruptly halted by a massive cracking noise. The whole building shuddered and shook.

Rebecca said: 'There was the odd scream. One father said "Out on the roof! " A tree had come into the building. A car might have come in as well. Most of the building had collapsed.'

Those looking on from the banks above the flood could see that the torrent had ripped away two thirds of the building, right up to the plasterboard front section of the loft where the families were huddling. Part of the slate roof hung down in front of it and that, as well as the tree, helped deflect some of the water from the crumbling structure.

Kim said that when the tree hit and the building collapsed, Luke began screaming 'We are all going to die now.' She tried to reassure her eight-year-old son that they were not going to die. But inside she shared just the same fear.

Melanie recalled: 'You could see daylight through the side of the loft wall – because there was nothing the other side of that – and water was seeping in there. I was aware by then that the wall had partly collapsed. The noise was incredible – banging, crashing. Like a bomb going off.'

Dave Pascoe

IF WE GET OUT ALIVE, I'LL NEVER SHOUT AT THE CHILDREN AGAIN

In desperation, the parents then devised a plan to save their children. They would get out on to the roof. Andy was first to climb through the skylight and position himself astride the ridge. From inside the loft, Alan lifted up the six children and passed them out one by one. Andy clasped their hands and pulled them up and over the wet slates to the apex. Because most of the roof had been washed away, there was perilously little room, so when Alan climbed out he dropped down to the lower adjoining roof of the toilet block and sat astride that.

Andy then lowered his sons Luke and Carl and the Graham twins Charlotte and Emily, down to Alan. Kim had also clambered out on the roof and she lowered her daughter Emily down to the toilet block ridge. Emily then couldn't move because she was so fearful.

Kim had to slide down backwards, in front of her daughter, and grip her by putting one hand behind her back and holding on to the roof with the other. Andy had no choice but to stay on the remains of the visitor centre roof with Rebecca Graham because the toilet block ridge could take no more people.

The water lapped up to the guttering just a few feet below them. Kim said: 'It was unbelievable. You could see trees and cars come down the valley. I shouted to Andy 'There's a tree coming down. I thought "If that hits us." '

Melanie, who is asthmatic, had tried to climb out of the window but couldn't get a grip. She froze with fear. She said: 'If I had put my hand out of the Velux window, I could have touched the water. All the trees had come down and were getting caught on every building. At the time we thought the building was going to collapse completely.' She remembers thinking: 'If we ever get out of this alive, I'm never going to shout at the children again.' She looked anxiously out of the window. With her now were Rebecca David and Beryl Walters, who lent Melanie her inhaler to help her get her breath.

Outside were the nine others, enduring the longest half an hour of their lives. The rain and hail froze their skin. They were soaked, shocked and fearful that the buildings would dissolve in the speeding water.

The crew members of RN Rescue 193
From left, Pete McLelland, paramedic Dave Pascoe, Mike Scott, Bob Yeomans and
Florry Ford (Culdrose Photographic)

One father clutching as best he could his twin daughters and two boys from another family. A mother clinging on to her daughter with one arm behind her back and the second father holding onto a child he had never met before that afternoon waiting for a helicopter to come and save them.

CHECK YOUR ORIENTATION POINTS IN CASE WE DITCH

The first military helicopter to reach Boscastle was Rescue 169, a yellow RAF Sea King from Chivenor, 50 miles away in North Devon. It took off at 4.15 pm and its captain and pilot Flight Lieutenant John Evans and his crew of three took 20 minutes to reach the stricken village. They arrived in the middle of a thunderstorm and he was startled by the scene below. He told the *North Devon Journal*: 'There was a dirty, dark brown raging torrent pushing everything in its path and I have never seen anything like it.'
Visibility was poor, it was raining and hailing, there were high winds going in all directions and lightning strikes on high ground. The crew were directed by the coastguard to a woman trapped in a building. The winchman, Sergeant Mario Testa, was lowered down and found the woman had lost a thumb and was bleeding heavily. John said that the coastguard then re-tasked them to someone having a heart attack, but the problem was attracting Mario's attention, so they fired a red flare into the water below to push something past the window. 'We left the lady and went to pick up the man and took him to the landing site where the (Cornwall) air ambulance was waiting to transport him to hospital. Our second crew later rescued the lady.'

At around the same time John Evans and his crew took to the air, Rescue 193, a grey and red Sea King from the Royal Naval Air Station at Culdrose, near Helston, also scrambled for Boscastle. The initial report was that a couple of people had been cut off in their cars by landslides and flooding. In West Cornwall the weather was still sunny.

Rooftop rescue. With the children safely in the helicopter, Kim Evans is winched aboard from the ridge of the toilet block. Her husband Andy can be seen sitting astride the remains of the visitor centre roof, gripping on and looking backwards. Alan Graham and winchman Bob Yeomans can be seen on the lower roof top (MoD)

Safe at last. The smiling faces of the Graham sisters, from left Charlotte, Rebecca and Emily among those rescued on board the packed Naval Sea King helicopter. Melanie Graham is sipping tea by the cockpit (Alan Graham)

The crew that day was led by Lieutenant Commander Florry Ford, a veteran of the first Gulf War, who would direct operations from the side door. Most of the flying was done by Lieutenant Mike Scott, directed by his co-pilot Captain Pete McLelland, who was on secondment from the Royal Marines. The winchman was Warrant Officer Bob Yeomans.

With a following wind, the 45-mile trip from Europe's biggest helicopter station took just 17 minutes. It was only when they saw the thick cloud over Boscastle and the state of the sea that they had any hint of the surreal scene to come.

Pete said: 'As we came from Port Isaac along the coast you could see various areas of sea where you would get a lot of rain washing off the land. It was a huge brown stain. The sea beyond was a beautiful green and then there was this perfect line like a half moon, which was completely brown.'

Their first job was to pick up a paramedic who had landed at Boscastle with the Cornwall Air Ambulance, the first aircraft of any kind to reach the scene that day. Dave Pascoe is an Assistant Divisional Officer for Westcountry Ambulance Service and over the last six years has flown many times with Culdrose, sometimes going down the wire as winchman. He knows the crew well.

They then searched around the harbour entrance to see if anyone had been swept out. Florry said: 'It was unreal. All I can remember is looking up the river and seeing this huge wave followed ten seconds later by all these cars. The wave almost stopped as the cars hit the harbour entrance, almost like it blocked for a second, and then the whole lot came through. It started as a torrent, then suddenly it was like a bulge.

The water was brown and white and full of trees and cars. It was getting churned and aerated. The rain was hitting the blades, running along the blades and running off. In 24 years in the service I have never seen anything like it.'

From the front of the aircraft, Pete was so concerned, he made a call he had never made before: 'I've flown all around the world but I have not seen rain like this. I remember saying to the crew "Can you check your orientation points in case we ditch." That's how bad it was.'

A DOG IN THE BACK SEAT WAGGING ITS TAIL

They were only about 200 yards from the RAF helicopter but couldn't see it because of the rain. As the flood spat cars out of the harbour entrance, Florry, Dave and Bob hung out of the door trying to see if there were people inside.

Florry said: 'Hazard lights were going. Windscreen wipers going. A lot of them were face or nose down.'

Then they saw movement in a blue Skoda and flew in for a closer look. It was a dog in the back seat, wagging its tail. Florry said: 'We wanted to go down but we had to make the decision that we couldn't go down for the dog because the next car may have had kids in it.'

Dave said: 'We all thought there would be people in the cars. The dog was just looking at us wondering what the hell was going on. That was sad – I'm a dog lover. We all felt the same. It was a heart-rending moment. All of us wished we could have done something.'

The flood was now at its most ferocious as the crew looked down in disbelief. Dave

The Graham Family (Melanie Graham)

The Evans Family (Kim Evans)

Florry said: 'We were still at 50 feet. Dave Pascoe then made the decision that this was a major incident. He asked that all available land assets be diverted to the area. So we called RAF Kinloss and declared it a major incident.'

At 5.10 pm on August 16, 2004, Captain Pete McLelland put out the call: 'Pass to all emergency services. This is a major incident. I repeat. This a major incident. We require all standby aircraft available and all available land-based emergency crews as we are in danger of losing Boscastle and all the people in it.'

THERE WASN'T A RIVER. THE FLOOD WAS THE WHOLE WIDTH OF THE TOWN

Florry could see boats being smashed into the harbour wall and water running up the road beside it. People were running away from the waves of the flood. He said: 'There wasn't a river. The flood was the whole width of the town. There were people waving, shouting, pointing.'

Pete said: 'We got a call from the coastguard mobile on the ground. He said "I've got some people in a house directly in front of me who are in danger of drowning." We didn't know where he was on the ground. I said "We have people all around us who look like they are in immediate danger." He says to me "You are just going to have to save whoever you can." I thought, "Bloody hell. This is serious." '

Their first airlift was a family of four visitors who had smashed their way through the roof tiles of a house near the bridge and were waving through the hole.

As they were winched up and the seconds ticked by in the gloom and mayhem,

continued: 'You could see this dark water now and the spread and power of it and what it's moving – buildings, cars, anything in its path – it's just destroying. I said to Florry "We will never see this again." It was a race against time. If you could see the power of this water, you were just waiting for the houses to be picked up and washed away.'

By around 5 pm most of the cars had been washed out. They could see the strobe of the first helicopter starting to move out of the valley to drop off the heart attack patient. As the Culdrose crew flew in over Boscastle village they saw people on the roofs.

something caught Pete's eye in the distance and caused him great concern. He said the first lift felt like an eternity because when he looked across to the visitor centre he could see two little girls with pink tops on, sitting on the roof.

BIG GRINS. MASSIVE GRINS

Just to make the situation even more hazardous, there were two sets of domestic power cables running in front and behind the visitor centre. Before flying up there they asked the coastguards to have the power turned off. Hovering above it, they could see the centre was taking the full brunt of the water and that the roof had peeled back. Florry recalled: 'You could see there were kids – and kids were the important thing. The adults were protecting them from the weather. They were sitting astride the roof ridge.'

Melanie Graham recalled the moment the helicopter arrived: 'The downdraft was incredible. My husband said that was the best part. He said that was warm. I watched the children go up into the helicopter. That was a great relief.'

View from the bridge. The dark waters sweep into lower Boscastle, smashing cars into buildings (Wayne Grundy)

Peter & Margaret Templar

Izzy (Kerriann Godwin)

laps. The girls were quite happy by then.'

The recovery was also a memorable moment for the crew. Florry said: 'As they got to the door I would embrace them to bring them in. The kids were scared coming up but the moment you had hold of them – big grins. Massive grins.'

Dave Pascoe recalled: 'They came in the aircraft with me and Florry. I sat them down individually. The children were amazing – there was one little blonde girl, her eyes were just popping out of her head.' The aircraft was getting short of fuel so Florry decided they would land at Boscastle football pitch high on a hill on the other side of the harbour. They told Falmouth Coastguards and RAF Kinloss that this would be the landing zone for the rescue operation.

Shortly before 6 pm 'Gold Control' was set up by Devon and Cornwall police to co-ordinate the incident.

Bob was lowered down to bring up the 12. The six children went up first. Because the strop was designed for adults, the children could have slipped out, so Bob supported them in it while bringing them up the aircraft. The six adults then followed.

Kim Evans said: 'Two of ours were the first to go and I remember putting my finger up to Andy to say 'That's one gone, that's two gone' – just sheer relief that one was safe and the other was safe. Then I said to Emily "There's a man coming down from the helicopter and he is going to take you up into it. You mustn't be scared. Do as he says. When you get up there give your brothers a good hug." ' When Kim got in the helicopter she cried. 'It was a relief that we were alive,' she said.

Melanie said: 'I was in shock by the time I got in the helicopter. They gave me some sweet tea. The children were all sitting on people's

Later, Florry would pause and reflect on a job which can mean taking lives and saving them. He said: 'I sank six ships with Sea Skua missiles. You are doing that and suddenly you are doing the opposite.' There is no question about what is the better job: 'I would definitely rather do Search and Rescue.'

Like so many of those airlifted that day, the Graham and Evans families went to the Rectory where they were greeted by the Rev Christine Musser, who found clothes for the children. Rebecca David put the Evans family up for the night. The Grahams got a taxi back to their caravan. Melanie said she didn't sleep that night and neither of them wanted to eat or drink.

Kim and Melanie have kept in touch since that day. They find it helpful to talk through the harrowing events of a day when they feared for their young families. Kim said: 'It helps having someone who went through it and knows how you feel. If we have a bad day we email or phone each other.'

She said of the helicopter crew: 'If it had not been for them, to this day we still say we would probably not be here to tell this tale.'

By the time August 16 was over, her words would be echoed by many more people.

A HUGE CRACK LIKE THUNDER. THEN A TIDAL WAVE

Between the first bridge and car park in Boscastle is a row of buildings known as Bridge Walk. When viewed from the helicopters that afternoon, it looked like a sprawling Elizabethan manor house enveloped by a vast, churning moat of trees, cars and racing water. It would become the centre of by far the biggest rescue in number as 55 men, women and children, and a German shepherd dog, were hauled up from the rooftops and neighbouring buildings in four lifts by a single RAF helicopter.

For several hours most of those people were trapped within Bridge Walk. Some who could see what was happening outside were fearful that the torrent which devastated the visitor centre just up from them would suck away the floors beneath their feet.

This is not one building but a complex at the heart of Boscastle commercial life. At the bridge end is the Riverside Hotel and Restaurant owned by Peter and Margaret Templar.

It is a sturdy structure built in 1584 by the Lord Lieutenant of Cornwall Sir Richard Grenville. At the opposite end is the modern Cornish Stores, owned by Guy and Tracy Lane-de-Courtin. In between is a small parade including Boscastle Bakery, owned by Sue and Nev Chamberlain, and John and Francilla Smart's Spinning Wheel Restaurant. At the back runs the river, and at the front is the main road through the lower village, which would be overrun by the flood. The shops are on the ground floor, with apartments and balconies upstairs overlooking the Valency.

By the time the river started to shoot up there were about 40 people in the Riverside's restaurant. Peter Templar recalled: 'The first I heard was a massive crack, like a huge crack of thunder. I reckon what had happened was that somewhere up the valley it had dammed up. It was as though somebody had just opened the floodgates because all of a sudden there was six or seven feet of water at the back of us. We have seen the river that high before but gradually. It was like a tidal wave filling it – like the Severn Bore.'

When the water started coming through the wall and the back door Peter ordered an evacuation: 'I shouted at the top of my voice "Everybody get out now!"

'The water was just coming up to the floor of the restaurant. There were families, children. Everybody left out the front. Most of them dispersed. They didn't have time to pay their bills.'

After smelling propane gas, Peter and Margaret and members of their family and staff, plus their pet dog Izzy, made their way through the flood water to the Cornish Stores. Peter believed they would be safest there because it was the only concrete building in the block. Peter said: 'Where the shop is, there was a big long straight wall. The water was hitting it and spilling out around the side. When we got out the water was raging. There was no way we could get across the road.'

Mark Saltern

Ken Goodman

IT'S MY CUP OF TEA AND I'LL DRINK IT

At the Spinning Wheel John Smart remembers being struck by the sheer noise of the river – and the strong smell of woodland coming into the restaurant. He said: 'Within a few minutes the water had risen to a ledge at the back of the restaurant which it had never done before. When I saw it was probably a foot deep around the front, I decided it was time to close. Most people had taken their cue from the water that was flowing from the back and started to leave, but one woman insisted on drinking her cup of tea because she had paid for it. She got up from the table and was downing the last half of her cup saying "It's my cup of tea so I'm going to drink it." Despite her worries about getting value from the £1.25 pot, she and the rest of the customers were evacuated.

At the village's only bakery Nev Chamberlain was cooking Eccles cakes when water started to seep in his back door. He recalled: 'We cook in batches of 18 and I had done about 15. I thought I'd better get these in the oven quickly so they can get cooked and I can concentrate on the water.' There were four in the shop at the time, Nev, Sue, and two employees, one aged 17.

I SAID TO THE BOYS 'I THINK WE'RE IN FOR A LONG NIGHT'

Delabole is six miles from Bridge Walk. Down by its renowned slate quarry is the fire station, which also serves its coastal neighbour Boscastle. This 'one-pump station' is manned by retained firefighters who all have jobs outside. They are a very close-knit team led by Station Officer Mark Saltern, a joiner, and Sub Officer Ken Goodman, a builder.

At 3.10 that afternoon, Mark, Ken and Firefighters Michael Davey, Dave Broad, Richard Bluett and Shane Trewin answered a call to go to Otterham Station, where they went to the aid of flooded householders. When they saw how bad the flooding was, Ken had a feeling about what was to come: 'I said to the boys, "I think we're in for a long night." ' Brigade HQ at Truro then told them they were needed at Boscastle and they made their way down roads running in two to three feet of water. When they arrived at the first bridge the sky was dim and the rain hammering down. It would quickly fill their regulation firefighters' boots. Mark recalled: 'First off we cleared the bridge. A lot of people were spectating. I said "If you've got somewhere to go – go". It was a dangerous situation. This storm was evil. People were getting soaked in seconds.'

IF IT WASN'T FOR THE FIREMEN WE WOULD HAVE BEEN SWEPT AWAY

The Delabole firefighters were joined by Roy Hooper from a Launceston crew, the first after them to arrive at the bridge. Mark requested he come with them as he is a first-aider. As the six went around the corner of the Riverside and up Bridge Walk, they left behind them driver Richard Bluett. It would be the last he would see of his friends and colleagues for several anxious hours. The water was then about knee high and flowing fast down the street.

Ken, a vastly experienced firefighter, said: 'At that point I had an awful gut feeling that once we entered in there we wouldn't be walking out. I went up to the wall outside the Cornish Stores and there was a lot of people sitting on it watching the cars. We told them to get off and get in. I saw the water sweeping in. I thought "This wall isn't going to last much longer." '

Mark Saltern then went looking for a phone to call fire control and when he walked past the bakery, he spotted the occupants at the back of the shop, fighting a losing battle against the water. He said: 'I opened the door. I saw them at the back of the shop, around the ovens, all standing with mops and buckets. I said "You're wasting your time. Make your way upstairs." I asked them if I could call fire control. I dialled 999. I said "A major incident is going to happen. We need more appliances Bude side of Boscastle because you can't get across the river." I had to keep it short because I saw three cars floating down the street. I said "I've got to go." The owner (Nev Chamberlain), came and helped me. He just managed to close the door behind me.'

Nev believes that if they hadn't followed Mark Saltern's command they would have been in serious danger. By this time the water outside the back windows was running at head height. He said: 'We had no idea that the water was going to get quite as high as it did. If it wasn't for the fireman coming in to use the phone and seeing the level of the water, we would probably have been swept out with it.'

As Mark left the building he was met by his number two Ken. The rest of the fire crew had gone into the Spinning Wheel where other people had also taken refuge in John and Francilla Smart's large apartment on the first floor. Mark said: 'From the time we

arrived on the bridge to the time we got indoors the water must have gone up six feet. This was just 10-15 minutes.' With no way back or across the flood, he and Ken made their way into the Spinning Wheel. They were the last inside Bridge Walk.

When vehicles started shooting down from the car park and crashing into the Cornish Stores, Peter Templar realised they were in danger again. He said: 'I saw about six recycling bins. They went down the river, bobbing up and down like synchronised swimmers. It was weird. Everything started hitting the wall of Guy's property.' He said he and Guy decided everyone had to get out. They went up to Guy's flat but the skylights would not open far enough. Peter feared that if the Cornish Stores collapsed, the whole block could go down like a pack of cards. He

grabbed a big drill and ripped the lead from it to use as a lead for Izzy the dog. Then he and Guy smashed a window. From the neighbouring skylight of the Spinning Wheel the firefighters could see they were trying to escape so Mark Saltern sent two of them out

Helen & Mark Saltern

to the roof. They were accompanied by a Boscastle man, Derek Nute, who volunteered to help out and was praised by both Mark Saltern and Peter Templar for his actions that day. The men helped the occupants of the Cornish Stores out of the window and across the roof. Ken said: 'As they came across, the fearful look on their faces was horrendous. Some had nothing on their feet and they were standing on broken glass. Some of the women were slipping on the slates.'

Mark said: 'I was thinking that something was happening with that building for them to come out so quick. One lady said that the building was shaking. I thought then that if the water got any higher, we were in deep trouble.'

IF I COULD GET THROUGH ON THE PHONE I WOULD RING MY WIFE – TO SAY GOODBYE

Some 22 people came out of the Cornish Stores and into the Spinning Wheel, swelling the number there to about 40. John and Francilla's was to become the departure lounge for the huge airlift that was to follow.

By now the flood water was reaching its peak at about six inches above the floor of the Spinning Wheel's first-floor apartment – meaning the encroaching surge was only held back by the patio doors. The occupants could see cars going past outside. Mark and Ken decided that everyone should move up to the

Four of the rescuers from the two RAF flights from Chivenor, from left: Sgt Mario Testa, MACR Steve Ward, Sgt Martin Thompson and Fl Lt Martin Wood. Between them the two crews rescued 58 people and a German Shepherd dog (Chivenor Photographic)

second floor loft area. Then there was an almighty surge of water and the ground-floor front door burst open. Knowing he had to stop the flood coming in and undermining the building, Ken climbed down into the water and with a huge effort managed to shut the door: 'I pushed my back against the stairs and my feet against the door and forced it. At that one point there I thought "Is this the end or no?" Basically, if a tree or a car had come through one of those patio doors, the force of that water would have engulfed that building inside, and we wouldn't have got the people out. You could feel the floor vibrating with the water. All we had was two panes of glass in that apartment between us and the water. I've been a firefighter 35 years this November. I've never seen anything like that. The flow. The debris. All the fires I have been in. I have never had that feeling before. We had no control over anything.'

The firefighters tried to keep people calm – especially the children. But Ken admitted: 'At one point I thought I would never see my family again. I was down the stairs watching these patio doors. It was frightening. It just kept rising and rising. I could see camper vans, cars, trees.'

Mark: 'I remember thinking "It's time for Plan B. But we haven't got a Plan B!" That whole block was at risk. We had mobile phones but they weren't working. I tried many times to call other personnel outside on my hand-held radio. I remember at one point I thought if I could get through, I would ring my wife to say goodbye, basically.'

Unknown to Mark at that moment, at the family home in Delabole Helen Saltern would be glued to the TV news as the drama of Boscastle unfolded, enduring the most anxious four hours of her life as she wondered what had happened to her husband and his crew.

Above the bakery, the four occupants were becoming increasingly fearful. Sue said: 'We were looking at the back. Looking at the front. My scariest moment was when I was on the balcony. All of a sudden something hit it so hard I thought it was going to collapse.'

Nev saw a fireman working his way along the balcony towards them. The officer asked them how many were in the building. At that point they did not know that the water had smashed through the back windows of the bakery beneath their feet. The flood had washed away everything including the massive oven with the cakes in it, and had created a waterway from the back of the building to the front as thousands of tons of water crashed through at an alarming rate. Nev said: 'We realised the windows had gone both ends because we saw freezers floating out. We didn't know but the Eccles cakes had gone.

'The ovens had gone. Everything had gone. The windows burst and took part of the wall with it. The back had gone. Our building was the only one with large windows and a door which meant it had weaker walls because there was less of it.'

DO YOU WANT TO KNOW A SECRET? I CAN'T SWIM

When Florry Ford's Navy aircraft hovered overhead, Mark signalled for them to go forward of Bridge Walk because he had seen there were people out on the roof of the visitor centre and toilet block who were in the greatest danger. The crew gave him the thumbs up.

The rescuers of Bridge Walk would arrive in the second yellow Sea King from Chivenor. The captain of the aircraft was Flight Lieutenant Martin Wood. In 24 years as an

As the floodwaters reach a pinnacle, by the Riverside Hotel a log-jam of vehicles swirls in the torrent. The red roof of the public phone box can clearly be seen. The booth would soon become another casualty as it was washed down-river (Don Stollery)

RAF pilot, he had never seen anything like the scenes unfolding around and beneath him. He said: 'When we went down the coast we had to go through three separate thunderstorms. There was a line of storms all the way down, static, for about 50 miles. The weather really was horrible.

'When we arrived at Boscastle I could see this torrent of water being split by the visitor centre. The water was breaking off the building like the bow of a boat. It was like liquid mud – brown dense and horrible. It was running above the ground floor windows.'

After Florry Ford's crew completed the rescue from the visitor centre, Martin Wood's

aircraft flew in to pick people off the big block of Bridge Walk behind it. Conditions could not have been more hazardous.

Martin said: 'We were hovering in torrential rain 20-25 feet above the roof with lightning flashing all around it and squalls and gusts of wind. It is dangerous to put a winchman down in those conditions but we had no choice. The danger is the cable can attract lightning. Some people had skylights or access to the roofs but others were leaning out of windows and Sgt Martin Thompson, the winchman, went in to get them. He got quite a few hugs and kisses that evening as he winched people up.'

Francilla & John Smart

Sue Chamberlain

At the Spinning Wheel window it was women and children first. Ken said: 'One woman was adamant she wasn't going to go out. I went over to her and said to her "Do you want to know a secret? I can't swim." She said "Neither can I." I said "Don't worry dear. We're in the same boat." I just grabbed her and her son and said "It's your turn. Go!" I kept saying to the women "Comb your hair before you go out because there will be TV crews." There was no hysteria. No screaming. We were there to help them.'

Among those waiting to be lifted were Peter and Margaret Templar, accompanied by their daughter Adrienne, her partner Shane, and their two children Amber (nine) and Kieran (seven). Margaret and Kieran were the first to be taken up – and a dramatic picture of the grandmother and grandson being hauled above the wide flood plane has become one of

the lasting images of the rescue.

Margaret said: 'I was the first one up with Kieran. That was after they rescued them for the visitor centre. The winchman came down and said "An adult and a child." I said "Come on Kieran, we're going." Kieran was fine. He said he wanted to do it again the next day. He had a big smile on his face.

'I have no fear at all but my daughter is terrified of heights. She grabbed my hand and said "There's no way I am going up in one of those." 'I said "If push comes to shove you are going up there." She came into that helicopter absolutely white as a ghost. She was petrified. She went up with Amber.'

Peter said: 'I went up with Guy. And Shane and Izzy followed us. They were the last. When she got up in the helicopter Izzy was as good as gold. I pulled her to me. She never flinched.'

John Smart said it was only when they were airlifted that they had a clear view of the building as an island in the maelstrom: 'One of the fire crew said that the only difference between us and them was that they were all wearing uniforms. No-one could be prepared for that event.'

Martin Wood's helicopter picked up 50 people in three lifts from the Spinning Wheel and neighbouring roofs. He said: 'They were very wet and shaken up but one thing that struck me was that their spirits were very high. I was amazed by their good spirits. When we dropped them off people were chatting to each other and hugging.

'My co-pilot Fl Lt Mark Dennis was talking to the coastguard and RAF Kinloss and controlling the other helicopters. The navy helicopters were searching the water while we were taking people off the roof and out of windows up to the football pitch.'

After completing the three lifts the crew flew to RAF St Mawgan to refuel. They then came back and rescued another five. They were the last air crew to leave the scene.

A PROPER FIREMAN'S LIFT

Mark, Ken and the rest of the firefighters sat it out in the Spinning Wheel. They were shivering cold, wet and hungry. Earlier Francilla Smart had been offering around a box of Cadbury's Roses. They decided it would be a shame to leave them, so the crew finished the box.
Mark said: 'As another helicopter got closer I said to the boys "I think this is our lift." '

Their rescuers were the crew of the Portland-based Coastguard helicopter, a Sikorsky captained by Kevin Balls. They were scrambled at 6pm and took 50 minutes to fly the 90 miles to Boscastle.

Like all the helicopter crews that day, Kevin was shocked and surprised when he arrived above the village. He said: 'A lot of debris had been washed out. The contents of people's house were spread all over the place.'

He added: 'It's the worst land-borne disaster we have ever attended. Most of what we do is yachts, dinghies and divers. Pulling firemen out of a Velux window was quite interesting!'

The Delabole crew were landed up to the football pitch. Their ordeal had lasted around three hours. Mark Saltern said it seemed like 30 minutes.

From there they hitched a ride in a coastguard vehicle back to the harbour, where they were reunited with their vehicle and driver Richard. He had endured a very anxious wait, seeing the flood devastate the lower village but with no communication with his team. Mark said: 'As we were walking down Richard turned around and he just beamed. He gave me one mighty hug and said "Am I glad to see you." '

Reflecting on the most testing job of their careers as firefighters, Mark said: 'I am convinced that we saved lives that day. That feeling is terrific. But in the same way, I did honestly think we were going to lose our lives.'

Ken felt the same: 'We had a lot of luck on our side as well. If that wall had gone when we were in the street, it would have taken the crew and a large number of people out.'

The four at the bakery stayed put and were eventually led out through the Spinning Wheel by another fire crew when the water had subsided. Nev said: 'We walked along the balcony. They took us through the back door of John and Francilla's flat. We went through the flat and down the stairs. The mud was really thick. Sue had a proper fireman's lift.'

Not long after the flood, Sub Officer Ken Goodman went on holiday to Turkey. When he came back he had some big news for his mates in the Delabole crew. At the age of 53 he had learned to swim.

DIVIDED BY THE FLOOD

Earlier, Graham King had been mightily relieved to see other people in uniform arrive as he manned the bridge. Ken Richards, the Station Officer of Port Isaac Coastguards, took over as officer in charge while Graham went to the upper part of the village to help organise the recovery operation there.

Graham said: 'It was great to see the helicopters – they were obviously needed.

They were taking casualties to the football field, then they were going to the Rectory. We borrowed a few vans and organised getting people from the Rectory to the Medical Centre, to the Village Hall so they could get checked out and have somewhere to go until the full emergency plan had kicked in.'

Kerriann was still on the other side of the water. Like so many people in Boscastle that day, she and Graham were divided by the flood. She eventually made it home to her cottage on the other side of the river very late that night. As the power was off, she put lighted candles in the window to let Graham know she was safely home.

I HAD EIGHT ON BOARD TELLING ME I HAD TO GET OUT OF THE HARBOUR

During their day at sea, Ken Cave and his party of anglers on board the *Boscastle Peganina* had a good day catching pollack, conger and ling. It had been calm, sunny and very hot but when he looked back towards Boscastle he could see black clouds hanging from Bude as far down as Padstow.

He got back to the harbour to be met by waves of brown floodwater laden with debris – fridges, tables, bits of tree, and the pile-up by the second bridge.

Ken said: 'I came right into the inner harbour straight away and then I saw it. I could see this mountain of trees. I could see my dinghy under the water. One boat was right under. I had eight people in the back telling me I had to get out.'

He turned around and headed out of the harbour, waiting offshore as the helicopters came in. Ken decided to head for the safe haven of Padstow, where the harbour master told him the news of the *Peganina's* home port.

The first lifeboat on the scene was from Port Isaac. When they arrived at Boscastle they were greeted by the surreal sight of a wave of water pushing as many as 50 cars in front of it. The water was thick with fuel as they smashed the backs of the floating cars to see if people were trapped inside. Lightning was striking around them. They found no-one.

The next day Falmouth Coastguards would be making broadcasts to shipping because there were cars and fridges and many other items floating up the coast between Boscastle and Hartland Point.

WHEN I WAS SWEPT AWAY BY THE FLOOD I THOUGHT 'YOU'RE DEAD'. THEN I HIT A TREE

On the afternoon of August 16, John Statton was working by the River Ottery, about a mile from the village of Canworthy Water, on the edge of the family farm. By road, this lush, tranquil vale is about ten miles inland from Boscastle – and a world away from the tourist honeypots of the north coast. The sturdy 63-year-old farmer and former captain of Launceston Rugby Club had his eleven-year-old grandson Lewis, working with him. They were taking down an old fence alongside the river and loading it on a trailer. The fencer, Martin Northey, was working further back along the banks. In the mid-afternoon, said John, the weather was lovely. Then they saw the river rising.

He recalled: 'We thought there must be rain somewhere. We could hear the thunder. The water was coming up to the top of the river bank. Then I saw it was the higher side of me.

By the miracle tree. Farmer John Statton at the River Ottery. In the middle of the picture is the forked oak which saved his life - the only one he could have grabbed as he was swept along in the flood

I said to Lewis "We'd better get out of here." '

As they drove back through the field they saw a white, four-wheel drive Daihatsu coming towards them. Inside were a couple from a neighbouring farm, Adrian Shute and Rebecca Eva, and their 15-month-old baby Senara. Adrian had come to warn John to shift cattle because of the rising water. John said that Adrian then decided to hitch up the low-loader trailer full of stakes and barbed wire to get that clear of the flood.

Very quickly the water came up and surrounded the vehicle, meaning Adrian couldn't drive away. John jumped on the trailer. When it started to shift in the torrent he decided to leap off – but found he was out of his depth in the flood water. By this time Lewis and Martin Northey were on the bank. 'They said I was swimming but whether I was or not I don't know now. I used to be a strong swimmer but I haven't swum much for years. I was in the water. I went along a bit and I could then stand on the ground. The water

was above my waist. Martin and Lewis went off to get help because they saw that we were really in trouble. After they'd gone I was swept away by the flood. When I got into the river I was under. I was fully clothed with Wellington boots on.'

By now the river was a 15-feet deep torrent and John was powerless as he was swept 60 feet from where he had been standing. He recalled: 'When I got swept away I remember saying to myself "You're dead. You can't survive in that water." I thought I'd had it.

'I was under water and I didn't know what was happening. But after that it was so quick. I hit the tree and it stopped me.'

The tree was a narrow, forked oak sticking out of the water now covering the far river bank. It was thinner than neighbouring oaks. John believes it was the only one there he could possibly have grabbed hold of because the others were too wide.

He said: 'I got my foot between the two forks

The dramatic scene as the RAF St Mawgan Sea King hovers over the River Ottery. The family of three huddle on the roof as their vehicle is swamped by the flood. On the bank, a fire blazes to guide the aircraft to the spot (David Paul Parsons)

and climbed up the tree. Then I thought, "Well, I've got a chance now." It's a miracle that tree was there. All the other trees were too big to hold. I saw the water was coming up and then I saw Adrian getting the three of them up and on top of the Daihatsu about 50 or 60 yards away. Trees were going down the river at speed. Miraculously the Daihatsu stayed there. I just put my arms around the tree and thought "I will have to stay here until the water goes down." '

John has trouble with his feet. He kept having to alternate them in the fork of the tree to keep his circulation going. 'I had a very tight pair of boots on. I couldn't kick them off – that was a good job because I couldn't have climbed the tree without them.'

From the top of the car Adrian was shouting to John – but he couldn't hear because of the roar of the river.

Earlier that afternoon Master Aircrew Clive Chapman, who would come to the aid of the four stuck in the flooded river, was at home near the coast when he saw the black curtains of rain.

The word torrential, he said, didn't describe it. Around 4 pm he drove to work at RAF

St Mawgan, near Newquay, and by 5.30 was flying towards Boscastle, having been scrambled by RAF Kinloss to join the rescue mission. Clive and the other four on board are all instructors and their usual role is to train SAR crews. Clive normally acts as winch operator but today his role would be winchman – for only the second time in his 22-year career. His fellow crew that day were pilots Flight Lieutenant Carl Holt and Squadron Leader Graeme Gow, winch operator Flight Lieutenant Niall 'Paddy' Rath, and Pilot Officer Mike Richards.

They flew to Boscastle and waited their turn to go in. As they orbited above the devastated village they got a call from Falmouth Coastguards requesting they go inland following reports of people hanging on to trees in the flood.

The flight to the River Ottery took just a few minutes and on the way Clive changed into his wet suit and took up position in the bosun's chair in which he would descend.

Their first rescue was of three people who had been trapped by the flood. Clive was winched down into the water to find a footing and got them on board. The three were dropped with a fire crew at Canworthy Water.

The coastguard then requested they go to a second incident in the main part of the river. When they got there one of the crew spotted smoke. Then they saw a group of about a dozen by the side of the river. The people had lit a big bonfire. Then they saw a car in the flood. The river was now about 30 metres wide and the car was in the middle. Huddled on top of the roof of the roof was a man, woman and small child – Adrian, Rebecca and Senara.

Rebecca told the BBC afterwards that Senara had kept saying 'water, water' and pointing to

it. She hardly cried at all. They kept her occupied by getting her to look at the sticks floating past and kept her warm by wrapping Adrian's overalls around her.

Clive recalled: 'The thing that attracted my attention was the force of the water coming down on this car. When you got a surge, the water was going up the bonnet and half way up the windshield.'

As the family on the car held on for dear life, the helicopter crew above them had a problem. Normally when rescuing babies and small children the winchman would hold them in his arms in a 'physical grip.' But this can be hazardous if the child is small, wet and slippery.

Graeme Gow came up with the solution – he suggested putting the baby in his rucksack. Clive recalled: 'I thought 'Ideal, absolutely ideal.' This is a standard issue, air force rucksack, about three feet high. I put a karabiner (a clip) through the shoulder straps and connected it on the rescue hook and tried it for size.'

Clive was now ready to make one of the most amazing – and hazardous – rescues of all.

He said: 'There were some trees at the rear of the car. We were about 70-80 feet above. I was winched out but started spinning around because of the rotor wash of the aircraft. I gesticulated to Paddy to just put me in the water. He carried me to the side of the car but I couldn't get a grip and the force of the water was pushing me away. Paddy decided to winch me clear. He carried me to the front of the car on to the bonnet. I was able to stabilise myself by kneeling on the bonnet with the water pushing me up against the windscreen.'

THE BABY WAS QUIET ON THE WAY UP. THEN SHE BURST INTO TEARS

Clive's first words when he got on the vehicle were: 'Hello, are you OK?'

He said: 'They nodded their heads. They were above the level of the water – just. The rotor wash was coming down on them and they were having to hold on. The baby was between them and was being held by the mother. I told them "I'll take the baby first." The mother said "Yes, fine." I opened the rucksack and said "Let's put her in here." She passed me the baby and I was feeding her legs in. I got her chest in and then tightened the pull cord. She had her arms and shoulders above the cord. She was calm, looking around taking it all in. It concerned me a little bit because she wasn't making any noise. The mum said "Take care of her. Have you got her?" '

Clive held on to Senara and told the parents 'I'll be back in a minute.' He was then winched up. Once through the door he passed the rucksack, complete with baby, to Paddy. Clive said: 'The child had been nice and quiet all the way up to the aircraft. When she realised her mum and dad weren't there she burst into tears.'

He went back down but then had even more trouble getting on the bonnet and kept being swept off. By now there was only about six inches between the flood level and the roof. 'The man (Adrian) grabbed my arm to help me on.

'We were having to shout to each other above the noise of the river and the aircraft. I ended up sitting alongside them on the roof. I told them "The baby is fine". I then put the mum into the rescue strop and did the toggle up and I was about to do the same thing for Adrian and he said:
"Don't worry about me, I'll stay here."
I said "No, you're coming with me."
He said that there was someone else in the trees behind the car.'

After taking up Rebecca and Adrian, Clive spotted a figure in the water hanging on to a tree.

The sight of the big yellow helicopter coming his way was a welcome one for John Statton. But as it got closer, for the second time that day he feared for his life.

He said: 'I thought when the helicopter came I'd had it then, because it was blowing the trees down. He couldn't get to me at first.'

Clive made several descents and was trying to break the branches off the tree to get closer. The main worry was dragging the hoist cable against anything. If it had broken he would have been swept away. On top of all that, he was aware that the aircraft was running very low on fuel – so he had to act quickly.

Clive said: 'I decided I had to get as close as I could and they winched me back into the water. We have a special extension lead which allows me to unhook directly from the winch hook but still be connected by six feet of webbing. I adapted this by attaching the strop to this lead and used it like a lasso, throwing the strop to the man at the base of the tree.'

As the minutes ticked by, the crew on board the aircraft realised they had enough fuel for just one last rescue attempt before they would have to leave.

After six throws, John Statton at last managed to get hold of the strop.

Clive said: 'We got clear with him dangling

six feet underneath me. We decided to carry him to the river bank. He reached the bank and as soon as his feet touched he took the strop off, gave me a thumbs-up and strolled away. He was fine. He was quite a cool customer.'

A grateful John said: 'It was marvellous what they did. Finally they got me out, on to dry land with everybody else.'

He had put his thumb up to Clive to let him know he was OK and joined the concerned crowd on the bank. John said: 'They had lit a fire. Martin Northey has a pretty new Land Rover and he put the spare wheel on the fire. He did marvellously. I was afraid they would try to come and rescue me in a tractor but it was so fierce a number of people could have been killed in this silly little incident.'

With an understatement typical of SAR crew, Clive Chapman said of the day's events: 'I happened to be in the right place at the right time.'

COLD, SHOCKED, BEDRAGGLED – BUT SAFE AT LAST

The village of Boscastle lies within two parishes, Forrabury and Minster, divided by the Jordan River. In the early afternoon of August 16, 2004, George Findlay, chairman of the parish council, was dodging thundery showers as he pottered between his back garden and garage. The retired farmer is also Tree Warden and a part-time postman, so he knows the topography and climate of Boscastle as well as anyone. George and his wife Jill live at the top of the hill near the church and their panoramic view of the highest cliffs in Cornwall and the Atlantic Ocean beyond mean they are well placed to watch the weather.

George Findlay

He recalled: 'I was thinking, "This is a hell of a storm at the back of us". And yet out to sea, the sun was shining. It was just about shining on the cliffs, which was unusual. I thought "This is the sort of weather that could cause a bit of a flood" – not thinking that it would be anything of the scale it turned out to be.'

His first warning of things to come was the sound of an alarm as the Delabole fire crew arrived. Then the Findlays had a phone call saying that the bridge was flooded. 'I said to Jill "It's not much good the chairman of the parish council up here supping tea when there's a big flood down in the village." '

He put on his weatherproofs and walked down. By the time he reached Marine Terrace at the back of the Wellington the level of the flood waters had reached the top of downstairs windows, and the Jordan had burst through the hotel.

He walked to the first bridge and was startled by what he saw: 'Cars and vans had started floating like ducks going down a stream, sitting right on top the water. I looked back at the Welly. The water was coming out of the windows and the door. There were beer barrels coming out the doors. A batch of trees came down the Valency. There must have

A wave of water surges down the main road bringing cars and debris with it, as firefighters wade in by the Riverside Hotel. On the opposite side of the road, people peer from a first-floor window (Wayne Grundy)

been several dams that had built up further up the river and they broke suddenly and came down. Another batch followed and hit the trees that were already jammed in the bridge. Those trees somersaulted over the bridge like so many acrobatic gymnasts over a vaulting horse. They were followed by a couple of cars. The rain came down in buckets, like tropical rain. It had drifted down towards us so we had a sample of what it was like up the hill.'

His first thought was for all the people wandering around, many of them visitors who were cut off from their cars and had nowhere to shelter. They were soaking wet and shivering in light summer clothing. He fought his way up the hill through streets which had now become rivers to fetch a key and open up the village hall.

On his way there he was partly responsible for the Boscastle flood becoming a major news event that evening. He recalled: 'When I came up from the lower region, I met David George of BBC Spotlight, who'd hitched a ride on a dumper trailer to get into the village. I jumped on the steps of the tractor and that was a wonderful opportunity for him to interview me in depth about what was happening down there. This was somewhere between five and six o'clock. David George couldn't believe what I was telling him. Before their evening news came at 6.30, he had a full account of what was going on.'

Another who could hardly believe his eyes that early evening was Wayne Grundy, an IT director and keen amateur photographer on holiday from Hove with his partner Helen Williams, a history teacher. He shot some now-famous video footage of the cars bobbing and weaving down the flood. The BBC bought the film and by the time the amazing images were broadcast on their main ten o'clock bulletin, the devastation of this tucked-away corner of a remote part of the

Wayne Grundy & Helen Williams (Wayne Grundy)

British Isles was well on the way to becoming worldwide news. Wayne was back at his hotel when a BBC producer first turned up and asked to have a look at the video. He recalled: 'He said "Let's see if we can get this down to the van and broadcast it on the ten o'clock news." I have to say this was one of my proudest moments. At 9.20 they viewed the video. We got back, sat in our room, put the TV on, and there it was.'

Before his own impromptu interview, George Findlay had phoned his wife and asked her to collect blankets and towels and ask neighbours to do the same.

Those evacuated by helicopter were dropped at Boscastle AFC football pitch. The vicar, Christine Musser, was there to greet the incoming flights. Despite the fact the Rectory had no power, she threw it open to the shocked and bedraggled crowds lifted from the lower village.

She recalled: 'It wasn't until about 4-5 o'clock when I started hearing the helicopters when we realised something was up. I met my parish reader Michael Parsons trudging up the hill soaked to the skin and he said "It's really dreadful down at the harbour. It's turning into a nightmare." That was the first knowledge I had because being up here on the hill we can't see down into the harbour.

'When the first helicopters landed at the pitch and I met the crews. I said, "Bring them here. Bring them to the Rectory. Let's get them in and get them dry." We were embroiled in it from then on.'

At the Rectory they were checked over by Dr Chris Jarvis, senior partner of the village medical centre, and then ferried by Christine down to the village hall.

George said: 'Lots of women and men came in to the village hall and helped to get things organised and made a list of people as they came in. We were overcrowded in the hall. There were well over 100 people there. Somebody had the foresight to know that we couldn't cope with everybody so Camelford Leisure Centre was opened up and there they put out the gym mats for people to sleep on.'

A coach was found for the rescued and stranded and two trips were made from Boscastle the five miles to Camelford. The Findlays also took in their friends Jane and Jim Castling, whose house by the harbour was badly flooded. Mr Castling was terminally ill when evacuated by Razor Keen, the winchman of Culdrose helicopter 194. Sadly Mr Castling died several weeks later. He was well liked and respected in Boscastle. He was involved with the Boscastle newspaper *The Blowhole* and in 2003 his guide to the village was published.

On the night of August 16, George Findlay was among several who drove to Camelford and offered to give people lifts home. He took a family back to St Merryn and didn't get home to bed until 2.30 am. That night he got two and a half hours sleep. Tuesday morning started off just like Monday – bright, calm and sunny. George Findlay walked down again, this time to see the devastation caused by the biggest disaster to befall his home village in all his 64 years.

(Don Stollery)

THE MIRACLE OF BOSCASTLE

The second bridge is totally hidden under a mountain of wrecked cars and trees, one of which looks like it has been planted by an almighty hand. Beyond the sad remains of the Harbour Light, and a Cornish flag fluttering in the breeze (Michael Parsons)

Driving to Boscastle on the morning of Tuesday, August 17, 2004, I felt a sense of trepidation. The overnight news had prepared me for a scene not only of widespread destruction but probably, multiple death. I thought back to a walk I had made up the north coast the summer before. I had stopped at a gift shop and chatted with the lady behind the counter about a 19th century painting of the harbour by William Gibbons, an artist from Devon, who was my wife's great-great grandfather. I had bought a couple of postcards of the print and as I left I reflected on how pleasant the lady had been, even though my purchase had been just loose change. This would be the last time I would

see the Harbour Light. The next time I would meet the owner Trixie Webster, the place she and thousands of others held dearly would be in ruins.

On the radio the figure reported was 15 missing. Almost inevitably, I thought, some of those would have been trapped in the cars swept down the village, a shocking scene captured by Wayne Grundy's video camera, or lifted off their feet by the flood and carried away. As I arrived in Boscastle, I asked a policeman if there was any update on the number missing.
'It's fifty now,' he said.
'I heard on the news fifteen – one five?' I said.

'No, I think it's 50 – five 0,' he said. 'You should prepare yourself going down there.'

Walking down the hill to the harbour I could hear the rush of the water and smell the silt. Helicopters still chattered overhead. I heard one woman bystander tell another forcefully: 'It's the Lord first. Don't let evil in.' I saw two male priests coming up, eyes to the pavement. Further down by the harbour the hot sun illuminated a scene of devastation. At the mouth, the tide receded to reveal mangled vehicles embedded in a swollen mass of grey silt, like pock marks on the side of a dead whale. A group of curious young men climbed down the rocks to have a poke around the car wrecks. Near the rubble of the Harbour Light flew a flag of St Piran. Trees stuck out like broken limbs from the windows of the Cornish Goodies shop. Its roof had a scar on it made by a floating car – testimony to how far up the floodwater had come. Covering the second bridge was a giant bird's nest of cars and uprooted timber as the water eddied around it. Further along, three cars were piled up on each other, like discarded Dinky Toys.

One of the great views of Britain had been turned into a scene resembling a battleground.

But as the hours of Tuesday, August 17, wore on there was the growing hope that maybe no-one was missing after all. The word 'miracle' was beginning to be whispered.

I WENT ABSOLUTELY BONKERS. I HUGGED THE CAGE

Included on one of the missing lists was a big, dark handsome chap called Eric, who had lots of admirers around Boscastle. Eric is Steve Lancaster's pet and the butter maker and his black cat lived in the lower village. Steve was

Steve Lancaster & Eric

working five miles away at the Dairy Crest plant in Davidstow on August 16. He couldn't drive home through the floodwaters so he walked all the way. Every step he was very worried for Eric. When he got to the bridge in Boscastle he could see across the flood that his ground-floor flat was surrounded by water. He said: 'Panic set in. I thought "That's it. He's had it really, he won't make this." Eric is my family. I'm divorced. Wherever I've gone, he's gone, which is why I felt this awful sense of betrayal, that I'd let him down.' After an anxious night staying at his landlord's house, on the Tuesday morning Steve went back down. It was, he said, an obscenely nice day. He wasn't allowed past the cordon but a fireman checked the flat and told him he couldn't find Eric. Steve said: 'That was it. Confirmation. I'm probably going to have to dig him out of the silt or he's been washed away.' Steve signed a register set up by the RSPCA and busied himself helping people carrying things and making cups of tea for the firemen. Steve said, 'Then at about half three in the afternoon suddenly there's a voice saying "Is there a Mr Lancaster here?" I looked behind me and there was a lady with a yellow hat on with RSPCA on it. I was a bit dazed. She said "We've found him." I can just remember going potty. I ran up and saw a menagerie of animals – they had lined them up by a little cottage near the Wellington. It was him. I just went absolutely bonkers. I cried but didn't get him out in case he did a

Many animals were trapped by the flood. The RSPCA launched a big rescue operation and among those recovered were dogs, cats, birds, hamsters, a rabbit, a rat - and even a goldfish in a tank (Les Sutton)

runner. So I hugged the cage.'

Eric's was perhaps the most amazing of all the animal escapes. He was found by RSPCA officer Claire Ford. The flood water had come within a few inches of the ceiling of Steve's flat, yet Eric's fur was clean. Steve said: 'I think that he must have been on the bed which then floated up to the ceiling with the water so he would have been pressed against the ceiling. That might explain why he wasn't dirty.'

With the help of the fire brigade the RSPCA rescued many animals, including two pairs of dogs, two cats including Eric, two aviaries of birds, two hamsters, a rabbit, Emily Maughan's pet rat Morpheus (she refused to leave neighbour John's house until a fireman went next door and checked to see if her pet was OK), a chinchilla – even a goldfish in a

tank. Chief Inspector Les Sutton, who co-ordinated the rescue, said: 'This was a valiant group effort between all the emergency services, all of who did an amazing job in very difficult circumstances.'

AN EEL TRIED TO SWIM INTO MY NEIGHBOUR'S HOUSE

The recovery of the animals was not the only glimmer of light in Boscastle the day after the flood. The spirit of the people, helping others in adversity, shone wherever you looked. At Marine Terrace, the row of 18th century cottages up the hill behind the Wellington, they were still battling the floodwaters 24 hours after the first 999 call. The Jordan, which runs through a culvert at the back, had smashed through their cottages and was still running outside their front doors. To add to

These grim images show the flood at its most ferocious. The downpour was at its peak and the noise of the water so great that people standing next to each other could hardly make themselves heard. The building in the foreground of the top picture is the Clovelly Clothing Company premises.

Part of it jutted out further than its neighbours and it was repeatedly hit by vehicles driven down by the torrent. The second picture shows the scene after it collapsed and was washed away. Richard Bluett, the Delabole fire crew driver who took the dramatic pictures, said: 'The rain was hammering down. If you look at the first picture you can see the pillar cracking. The water was pressing on the wall. Once the wall went the roof came in. It was only about ten minutes between the two pictures.'

Richard had a long and anxious wait, not knowing where his crewmates were after they had walked over the bridge and around the corner. Before the building was undermined, two Clovelly Clothing staff made their way safely into Bridge Walk and were airlifted. One, the manager, saw his new BMW float past on the flood. He was one of many who either watched their cars carried away as it happened or later saw TV footage of them being driven down the streets at speeds well in excess of the limit. The BMW was eventually found washed up at Trebarwith Strand (Richard Bluett)

their problems, the heavy rain returned. Teams of volunteer helpers had come down to the terrace to help the householders sandbag their properties against the flood. As they piled up the bags to try to keep the water out, they were soaked to the skin and running on the last dregs of energy but still they dragged themselves up and down the steep hill.

Raymund Rogers, the acclaimed Boscastle artist, who lives in Marine Terrace, was deeply moved by the community coming together. The previous day he had been painting in his loft when the flood hit. He came downstairs to salvage property and ended up virtually swimming in chest-deep water as his furniture floated up to the ceiling. He has nothing but positive memories of the aftermath. He said: 'I think if I cried it was with tears of joy at being so blessed, seeing so many of the community hands on with shovels and rakes, doing this work. I counted about 24 people in the house in one day. Several of them I have never seen in my life before. They were getting all the muck and dirt out. There was a great sense of

optimism. Boscastle has always been a very close-knit community. It has become even closer still.'

His artist's eye was also gladdened by nature: 'I saw a yellow brimstone butterfly which I had never seen in Boscastle before. And the bees fluttering about. Nature was just carrying on in the midst of all the chaos. And I saw an eel swimming up the river here and desperately trying to swim into my neighbour's house!' When positive-thinking Raymund suggested that the silt washed down the valley would enrich the soil for growing vegetables, he received several packets of seeds through the post.

THOUGH YOUR HEART BE BROKEN, RISE AGAIN

Wednesday is the night the singers of Boscastle gather at the Wellington Hotel. Raymund Rogers and Graham King suggested to John Maughan, the Boscastle Busker, that they should still go down two days after the

Roads ripped up, buildings washed away. The devastation caused by one of Britain's worst-ever floods is graphically illustrated in this picture taken beside the first bridge two days after the event. An estimate of the total damage has put the bill as high as £50 million (Richard Bluett)

flood and have their traditional session, even though the hotel had been seriously damaged. It would be a homage to the Welly. Three or four dozen gathered outside for what was to be an emotional and healing experience. The song which had the most resonance and which, they say, epitomised the spirit of Boscastle is a ballad about a shipwreck called *The Mary Ellen Carter*. Its rousing final lines are:

> *Rise again, rise again – though your heart*
> *it be broken*
> *And life about to end*
> *No matter what you've lost, be it a home,*
> *a love, a friend*
> *Like the Mary Ellen Carter rise again.*

As he sang, John looked around at the other singers. Some of them had lost a great deal indeed. John said: 'Their eyes were welling up. But they knew that they would rise again. It was sung with great gusto.'

I'VE LOST MY HOME. BUT THE SPIRIT OF THE VILLAGE IS PHENOMENAL

In the days after the flood, more amazing accounts of bravery, escape, kindness and loss began to emerge from August 16, 2004.

On the day of the flood Scott Roberts of the Wellington was left shocked and upset when he managed to drive the long way around from the car park to the other side of the river

Raymund Rogers

Luke and Jeorjia Gifkins (Mod)

and found his family's hotel so badly damaged. Scott's flat was on the first floor and had collapsed. He lost virtually everything he owned as the water and mud poured through, including most of his 500-strong collection of cookbooks. However, he was cheered immensely when eventually his girlfriend Suzanne's great grandfather's wedding ring, two rings he had given Suzanne, and his grandfather's sovereign ring turned up in the painstaking search of the three-feet deep silt at the back of the bar.

Gay Truswell was airlifted from a friend's roof. Later that night on the TV news she watched the motorhome in which she lived floating out on the flood. Virtually everything she owned was in it. She told the *Nottingham Evening Post*: 'To see it dancing backwards down the river was incredible. It was as if it had no weight at all.'

She added: 'I've lost my mobility, my home and I've lost my treasured family photographs and sentimental things. But the spirit of this village is phenomenal.'

A picture of the rooftop rescue of father and daughter Luke and his 14-year-old daughter

Jeorjia Gifkins became one of the iconic images of the disaster. Luke, a tree surgeon from Hertford said: 'The first thing we saw that made my stomach turn was that all of a sudden this red car went bouncing down the river really fast with its lights on, upended, and stuck against the bridge. This is what caused all the problem. It blocked the flow of water. Then trees and debris were coming down and sticking by it. If that car hadn't stuck under that bridge, then the water could have flowed out to sea. We were standing on the roof for quite a while. My daughter said "Dad, the building's going to collapse." The noise I couldn't describe to you. I had her cuddled inside my Barbour coat and I was holding on to her as hard as I could. I said "No it's not, these buildings have been here for 300 years." She was fine when she got up in the helicopter. It was the noise factor. She wanted to get away from the noise.'

Tony and Barbara Upton and their son John, from Doncaster, were stranded in Boscastle after their car was swept away. Hearing of their plight, Michael and Patsy Burton, from Essex, gave them £2,000 to buy a replacement – money they had raised from selling video footage of the flood to a TV company.

Aftermath. As the waters recede and sunshine returns to Boscastle, the full force of the flood can clearly be seen. Trees protrude from the windows of Cornish Goodies as members of the rescue services survey the scene (Don Stollery)

WORLD NEWS

Less than two hours after the streets of Boscastle were first hit by the flood, the disaster was worldwide news. Agencies flashed the story around the globe and it made headlines in many countries, including China, France, Canada, Australia, the USA and India.

In the UK, dramatic pictures of the flood were broadcast by the BBC, ITV and Sky, and in New Zealand, among other places, it was a lead item on the TV news.

By the following morning, Boscastle was swarming with journalists as major news networks and national papers sent top reporters and cameramen to cover the story. The result was saturation coverage in the national, regional and local media. The sense of amazement and great relief that nobody died was reflected in a headline in the *Daily Telegraph* on August 18 which said: 'Villagers saved in the 'miracle' of Boscastle.'

FIFTY TWO YEARS ON

Then there were the uncanny parallels between the North Cornwall floods on the afternoon and evening of August 16, 2004, and the famous Lynmouth flood disaster which happened on the night of Friday, August 15, 1952. The circumstances were similar in that in both cases a cloudburst occurred over a steep valley and the ensuing flood caused massive damage. Those who look for these things found other co-incidences. The year 2004 is 52 years after

1952. The two places have similar post codes. Boscastle's is PL35, Lynmouth's EX35.

Though the dates coincide, there is no comparison in human terms. As Eric Delderfield recorded in his book *The Lynmouth Flood Disaster*, in that catastrophe, 34 people were killed or missing, 93 houses and buildings were destroyed or subsequently demolished, 28 bridges were destroyed or badly damaged and 132 vehicles were destroyed.

The statistic that mattered more than any in the 2004 flood was of course that not a single person died. It is generally accepted in Boscastle that two dogs were washed out in cars. Four buildings were destroyed by the flood or subsequently demolished – Boscastle Visitor Centre, plus three shops, Things, Clovelly Clothing and the Harbour Light. North Cornwall District Council reported that 58 homes were affected by the flood, 25 of which were second homes. Seventy-nine cars were recovered from the village and the inner and outer harbours. Alfie Biscombe said that four bridges up the Valency Valley had been washed away.

Cornwall County Council reported that fire control staff took more than 100 calls in the afternoon, rising to 170 in the early evening, from people trapped in buildings, cars and trees. Seventeen vehicles and more than 100 fire service personnel from Cornwall and Devon were at the scene in the evening. Some 150 staff from the fire brigade, highways and emergency planning departments worked through the night.

On the evening of August 16, North Cornwall District Council set up an incident room and an emergency call centre at Wadebridge. Hundreds of calls came in, many from people worried about relatives on holiday in the area. There were many offers of

Smart suit and wellies: A TV reporter gets the lowdown after descending the rocks to stand among the silt and debris of Boscastle Harbour (Aaron Wood)

help from around the country.

The council's building control team played a crucial role in checking the stability of all the buildings and recommending which ones should be demolished or shored up and made safe. The operational team were there from the start to help with the clear-up.

Once police handed control over to the council's chief executive, David Brown, on the Thursday lunchtime, he was in charge. He chaired 'silver control' meetings in Boscastle and then held residents meetings to keep people informed. Mr Brown's role was to lead and co-ordinate the whole clean-up operation and hand over the site safely to residents. The council also set up a business task group to help the financial recovery and are now spearheading regeneration work.

The authority also worked closely with the National Trust, a major land and property owner in Boscastle. Trust properties in the harbour area, the roads leading to it and the riverside walls were all damaged. An early report suggested the harbour wall had suffered impact damage. The flood also affected farmland and coastal paths and caused considerable damage to the Valency Valley. The footpath up the valley was closed as parts of it had been washed away.

One estimate of the cost of the flood damage to insurance firms put the bill as high as £50 million.

ONE OF THE BIGGEST FLOODS EVER RECORDED

No-one in the vicinity of the Valency, Jordan or Ottery on August 16, 2004, needs to be told there was a quite phenomenal weather event that day. Just how extraordinary was confirmed in a report made public by Environment Agency flood defence managers in early October 2004. Early indications were that the flood ranked among the most extreme recorded in Britain. The report said that the heaviest rainfall fell along a line generally corresponding to the A39 Atlantic Highway to the east of Boscastle.

This runs along the high ground separating the River Valency and the Crackington Stream to the west, the River Camel to the south, the Rivers Inny and Ottery to the east and the River Neet to the north.

Most of the rain fell in the four hours from 1.30 pm. The highest measured rainfalls for the 24-hour period were 200.4mm (nearly eight inches) at Otterham and 184.9 mm (just over seven inches) at Lesnewth. George Findlay's rain gauge in his garden at Boscastle showed just two inches, meaning the rainfall up the valley was around four times that which fell on the village.

Kerriann Godwin with a dummy of Joan the Wisewoman, one of the most popular exhibits at the Museum of Witchcraft. Kerriann said: 'She really gave the firemen a fright when they came in to check if there were any bodies, because she was lying on her back looking all pale and pasty, rather like a corpse.' Among other cherished relics painstakingly recovered from the silt was Harry the tarred head

In comparison, the highest recorded rainfall on August 15, 1952, above Lynmouth was 228.6 (nine inches) over a period of about seven hours.

The paper noted 60 properties flooded in Boscastle. About a further 40 were flooded in Canworthy Water, Bude, Helebridge and Crackington Haven.

There was also some good news for the people of Boscastle. The agency decided to immediately replace the culvert behind Marine Terrace and upstream of the Wellington and said the work should be completed by December 2004. However, the agency said the work would reduce the risk of flood 'but inevitably will be overwhelmed by extreme conditions like 16 August 2004.'

David Crichton, Visiting Professor at the Benfield Hazard Research Centre at University College, London, said that not only was the date the same as at Lynmouth, 52 years earlier, the circumstances of the Boscastle flood were similar to Lynmouth, in that it was caused by a heavy localised rainstorm over a steep catchment.

He said: 'The heavy rain was caused by westerly winds carrying the remnants of Hurricane Alex, which had picked up vast amounts of water from the Atlantic on its journey towards the UK. Winds hit the peninsula of Cornwall from the sea to the North and South of the peninsula, converging over the hills in the centre of the peninsula, pushing clouds up to 40,000 feet high. This produced a prolonged, stationary thunderstorm resulting in 130mm (6 inches) of torrential rain in six hours (the monthly average is 70 to 90mm).

Prof Crichton added: 'Fortunately there were no deaths or serious injuries, probably mainly because the event happened during daylight and near an RAF base, a Royal Navy base, and an HM Coastguard base each with rescue helicopters and highly trained search and rescue crews who were at the scene within 20 minutes of the first notification. They did an amazing job. However the effects of shock after such an event could be long lasting.'

THE 'MIRACLE OF BOSCASTLE'

When I met College Fletcher at his flood-damaged home he was still weary from the shock of the flood. He told me: 'I've been emotional. I have been through shock, a fire, I got a lad called Graham out of his bedroom in Keswick, so I kind of know all about it. It does hit you about two or three days after and lasts for about a week. There have been some grown men crying.' To be sure, a lot of people in Boscastle needed a good stiff drink by the end of that Monday.

His neighbour Wanda Larratt is a nursery assistant at the village primary school just down the hill. While some other small coastal communities hibernate in the winter, Boscastle is proud of its school and the vibrancy the children bring to the place. I met Wanda the day I met College and she said the flood had affected different people in different ways: 'On the actual day that it happened, at that moment it was the women in tears, crying, and it was the men who did the rescue and were coping. Since then some of the men have been reduced to tears. I think we're all pretty strong here. Everyone will be OK in the end. Boscastle will come back. We don't see any other option.'

Wanda was far from the only person I have met who described the fact that no-one died as a miracle. Peter Templar used the same word. So did George Findlay, Martin Wood Steve Lancaster, and many others. In the media the event quickly became 'The Miracle

Wanda Larratt

Christine Musser (Jim Castling)

Perhaps even more astonishingly, not one single person seems to have been caught in the flood up the Valency, one of the best-walked valleys in Cornwall, especially in August. The theory in the village is that the deluge must have driven them away before the flood peaked.

Trixie Webster is not alone in believing there was a guiding hand that day. When I met her she was continuing clearing up her damaged home with the help of friends. Just across the river stood a pile of rubble, all that remained of the Harbour Light.

She said of the day of the flood: 'I felt His presence. And I've felt it ever since. I think that's why I haven't really gone into depression or a feeling of bereavement. It has been like a bereavement but it didn't go that deep. I just trust Him. I believe there was a guiding hand. It was a miracle there was no loss of life. There's a community spirit here. This village has always been fairly close. But it's closer now than it's ever been. I believe that if we can maintain that with each other, good will come out of it.'

of Boscastle' and for once, the use of such an emotive word didn't just seem like newspaper hyperbole. What people could not fathom was how in an area containing perhaps as many as two thousand people that day, not one was dragged away and claimed by the flood. Those in the helicopters know that if someone had been pulled in, their chances of survival even in a lifejacket, were minimal. Yet not one of those 79 cars had anyone in it when they were washed down village streets faster than the legal speed limit. A building in Boscastle had been identified for the bodies the emergency services feared would be found. The delivery of body bags was being arranged. Mercifully, these grim measures were not needed.

Sue Chamberlain of the bakery has not lived in Boscastle very long. Now she can't imagine leaving. She said: 'I'm not the sort of person to get upset about property. If somebody had been killed that would have been awful. So we have lost the bakery? I couldn't cry over it. It will get rebuilt. But no-one got killed. The one thing that has made me want to cry is everyone putting their arms around me and saying "How are you?" But when I am down at the building, I just think "What a blinking mess." We have made so many friends since this disaster. The following day we went to Wadebridge to buy some Wellingtons and we went into Boots. One woman broke down in tears when I told her I was from Boscastle. We've had people sending us letters with cheques in.' One woman from Liverpool sent Sue and Nev a

£50 note so they could have a night out.

Whichever way you look at it, miracle, or just a freakish catastrophe alleviated by huge measures of bravery, skill, and good fortune, there is little doubt there would have been loss of life but for the quick thinking of many people both in and out of uniform in North Cornwall on August 16, 2004, some of whom appear in these pages.

Dave Pascoe has seen a lot in his 27 years in the ambulance service. But he had never seen anything like the flood. He said: 'These guys in the Search and Rescue aircraft, they are truly worth every penny. If it wasn't for those aircraft there would have been so many people killed, without a doubt.'

In the days following the flood, Christine Musser saw her main role as a listener for anyone who wanted to talk about what they had been through and to get it off their chest. She said: 'I think everybody was struck by this sense of unreality. It's only by telling the story and retelling it that it starts to sink in, the reality of what's happened.'

She believes that the strength of the community was borne out by the way people reacted to the crisis which befell them on August 16. She said: 'I think Boscastle people have taken it very well. It is a close community. It's a small community. North Cornwall can be quite an isolated place. You feel a bit cut off from the centre of things sometimes. So they do tend to pull together in times of crisis. Nobody could have imagined a crisis on this sort of scale. It is a marvellous place to be. I feel privileged to be part of such a community. Neighbours take in strangers and friends alike and share what they have got and rise to the occasion and meet whatever needs are there. That was very very apparent, particularly in the first few days and weeks. But that continues. I think people are supporting each other to the best of their abilities really.'

She, too, is happy with the word miracle. Christine said: 'I can use that word and I think it's entirely appropriate. There were so many close calls. You think "How on earth did everybody manage to get out of that?" Certainly around here, we have the greatest respect and admiration for those helicopter guys.

'The bravery, continually flying in those conditions and getting all those people out, was incredible.'

(Richard Bluett)

THE MAGNIFICENT SEVEN

Seven helicopters airlifted 100 people in Boscastle and neighbouring areas of North Cornwall on August 16, 2004. The first RAF Sea King was airborne from Chivenor at 4.15 pm, and was joined by a second from the North Devon base, three Sea Kings from the Royal Naval Air Station at Culdrose, and a sixth manned by instructors from RAF St Mawgan, near Newquay. The Coastguard helicopter from Portland, Dorset, was the last aircraft to join the mission, making up 'The Magnificent Seven'. Cornwall Air Ambulance also assisted. When it looked as though as many as 1,000 people could be in danger, a Chinook heavy lift helicopter flew from RAF Odiham, Hampshire, to St Mawgan, but was not used in the airlift. So successful was the mission, the RAF say it will be a benchmark for future operations of a similar scale.

(Aaron Wood)

Rescue 193 (Culdrose): Lt Cdr Florry Ford, Captain Pete McLelland (Royal Marines), Lt Mike Scott, Warrant Officer Aircrewman Bob Yeomans. Recovered a family of four through a hole in a roof in the harbour area. Recovered two families of five, the manager, and a volunteer, at Boscastle Visitor Centre. Airlifted a SAR Commander. Recovered four Firefighters. Total assisted – 21.

Rescue 194 (Culdrose): Flt Lt John Everitt (RAF), Ldg Aircrewman 'Cags' Lacy, CPO Aircrewman 'Razor' Keen. Initially recovered two casualties from area south of village, then searched offshore for survivors and later searched inland for persons in distress. Assisted a medical casualty in a house adjacent to the harbour. Winchman and stretcher lowered to back garden, casualty delivered to land ambulance at Boscastle football pitch. Total assisted – 3.

Rescue 195 (Culdrose): Lt Cdr 'Tank' Murray, Lt Cdr Jerry Barnbrook (Sqn CO), Lt Tim Barker, Ldg Aircrewman Jason Bibby. Searched around coast, nothing found. Transferred paramedic to Boscastle, then flew woman with chest pains from Boscastle to Treliske Hospital, Truro. Refuelled at St Mawgan then returned to Boscastle to drop off one doctor. Total assisted – 3.

Rescue 169 (Chivenor): Flt Lt John Evans, Co-pilot Flt Lt Victoria 'Tor' Turnbull, Radop Flt Sgt Dave Sheppard, Winchman Sgt Mario Testa. Rescued man with suspected heart attack. Dropped him at football field with Cornwall Air Ambulance. Sent on two searches for people

(Aaron Wood)

in cars – nothing found. Sent to pick up two people stuck on roof at Marhamchurch. Total assisted – 3.

Rescue 170 (Chivenor): Flt Lt Martin Wood, Co-pilot Flt Lt Mark Dennis, Radop MACR Steve Ward, Winchman Sgt Martin Thompson. Lifted 50 people and a dog in three lifts from the roofs and upstairs windows of buildings cut off by the water. Went for a refuel at St Mawgan and returned to pick up a further five. Total assisted – 55 and a dog.

Rescue 180 (St Mawgan) Captain: Flight Lieutenant Carl Holt, Co Pilot: Squadron Leader Graeme Gow, Radar/Winch Operator: Flight Lieutenant Paddy Rath, Winchman: Master Aircrew Clive Chapman, Supernumerary: Pilot Officer Mike Richards. Recovered three people from a tree at Canworthy Water. Rescued a family of three from the roof of a car in the flooded River Ottery. Recovered man from tree in the river. Flew to St Mawgan to refuel. Master Aircrew Mike Cornes took over as winchman from Clive Chapman. Recovered two people with mild hypothermia from Boscastle to North Devon District Hospital, Barnstaple. Total assisted – 9.

(Aaron Wood)

Coastguard helicopter (Portland): Pilot Kevin Balls, Co-pilot Richard Tye, Winchman Paul Mansell, and Winch Operator Roy Eggleston. Did a sea search up and down the coast a mile or two either side of the harbour entrance. Recovered six firefighters from a window at the Spinning Wheel restaurant, Boscastle. Did an infrared survey of cars to see if anyone was trapped. Refuelled and checked other villages. Total assisted – 6.

ACKNOWLEDGEMENTS

The author would like to thank the people of the Boscastle area, members of the rescue services and all others who have given their assistance.

In particular, Philippa Arthan, Kevin Balls, Rick Barnett, Jo Barr, Alfie Biscombe, Richard Bluett, Jane Castling, Ken Cave, Fred Caygill, Nev Chamberlain, Sue Chamberlain, Clive Chapman, Mark Clark, David Crichton, Charlie David, Rebecca David, Mike Dunning, Pat Edgar, Andy Evans, Kim Evans, George Findlay, Jill Findlay, Dave 'College' Fletcher, Molly Webber, Florry Ford, Doreen George, Kevin Gibbs, Luke Gifkins, Kerriann Godwin, Ken Goodman, Alan Graham, Melanie Graham, Davinia Grist, Wayne Grundy, Sarah Hancock, Janet Hopkinson, John James, Douglas Johnson, Craig Jones, Malcolm 'Razor' Keen, Graham King, Barbara Kilby, Steve Lancaster, Wanda Larratt, Myrna Lester, Cheryl Maughan, Emily Maughan, John Maughan, Ian Mackay, John McLaughlin, Nadine McLaughlin, Rob Matson, Pete McLelland, Annie Moore, Levannah Morgan, Michael Mulford, Christine Musser, Shona Owen, David Paul Parsons, Michael Parsons, Ruth Parsons, Dave Pascoe, Bernie Pettersen, Simon Rabett, Paul Roberts, Scott Roberts, Raymund Rogers, Helen Saltern, Mark Saltern, Rebecca Shute, Fred Siford, Francilla Smart, John Smart, Kate Smith, Matthew Smith, John Statton, Mel Statton, Don Stollery, Rachelle Strauss, Richard Strauss, Caroline Sutton, Les Sutton, Carole Talboys, Richard Taylor, Margaret Templar, Peter Templar, Chris Thomas, Graham Tiplady, Dave Webster, Trixie Webster, Aaron Wood, Martin Wood, Tim Wood, Jono Wardle, Ken Whitfield, Bob Yeomans

Also thanks to Adrian Baker, Heather Corbett, Ivan Corbett, Florence Lawrance, Steve Rayner, Kathy Rowe, Melisande Rowe and Mike Rowe, for their expert assistance.

To anyone else who has helped and been accidentally omitted from this list – my apologies and sincere thanks.

David Rowe, November 2004.